Under the Starry Night

A Wayfarer's Guide Through
An Uncertain World

Under the
Starry Night

Dennis Billy, C.SS.R.

AVE MARIA PRESS   Notre Dame, Indiana 46556

© 1997 by Ave Maria Press, Inc.

International Standard Book Number: 0-87793-614-5
Cover design by Elizabeth J. French.

Cover art: van Gogh, Vincent. *The Starry Night* (1889). Oil on canvas, 29 x 36 1/4". The Musuem of Modern Art, New York. Acquired through the Lillie P. Bliss bequest. Photograph © 1997 The Museum of Modern Art, New York.

Excerpt from *Crime and Punishment* by Fyodor Dostoesky, translated by Sidney Monas. Translation copyright © 1968 by Sidney Monas. Used by permission of Dutton Signet, a division of Penguin Books USA Inc.

Excerpt from "The Hollow Men" in *Collected Poems 1909–1962* by T. S. Eliot, copyright 1936 by Harcourt Brace & Company, copyright © 1964, 1963 by T. S. Eliot, reprinted by permission of the publisher.

Printed and bound in the United States of America.

Library of Congress Cataloging-in-Publication Data

Billy, Dennis Joseph.
     Under the starry night : a wayfarer's guide through an uncertain world / by Dennis J. Billy.
          p.   cm.
     Some parts of this book previously published elsewhere under various titles between 1992 and 1996.
     Includes bibliographical references.
     ISBN 0-87793-600-5. — ISBN 0-87793-614-5 (pbk.)
     1. Spiritual life—Catholic Church. 2. Catholic Church—Doctrines. 3. Billy, Dennis Joseph.   I. Title.
BX2350.2.B53   1997
248.4'82—dc21   96-44076
                                         CIP

In memory of
my grandparents,
Nicholas and Mary Billy
Joseph and Anna Miano,
who traveled homeward
by the light of the starry night

This book will make a traveller of thee,
If by its counsel thou wilt ruled be.

John Bunyan, *The Pilgrim's Progress*

Contents

Acknowledgments

Parts of this book have been published elsewhere under the following titles: "Under the Starry Night," *New Blackfriars* 76 (1995): 43-48; "Wandering Through Lent," *Pastoral Life* 43 (no. 2, 1994): 36-40; "The Abbey of Sénanque: A Journey of the Heart," *Review for Religious* 54 (1995): 716-22; "The Mark of Cain," *Pastoral Life* 43 (no. 9, 1994): 37-39; "Marked by the Ashen Cross," *Pastoral Life* 42 (no. 2, 1993): 37-39; "Conversion and the Catechism: Echoing the Faith for Others," *Journal of Spiritual Formation* 15 (1994): 197-209; "Friends for the Journey," *Living Prayer* 29 (no.1, 1996): 13-18; "Passionate Prayer," *Living Prayer* 29 (no. 2, 1996): 3-7; "Fostering Spiritual Friendships," *Pastoral Life* 41 (no. 4, 1992): 2-9; "Called to Community," *Review for Religious* 54 (1995): 371-82; "Re-imagining God," *Living Prayer* 28 (no. 1, 1995): 23-29; "Secret Stars," "cain," "The Traveler's Rest" in *As There as the Sky* (Whitby, ON: The Plowman, 1995), 13, 16-17, 26. A word of thanks goes out to these journals and publishers for allowing me to incorporate these pieces into a larger work.

Special thanks also go to Robert M. Hamma and Holly Taylor Coolman of Ave Maria Press for their invaluable editorial advice and technical assistance.

Introduction

How many of you have ever looked out under the dazzling canopy of stars of a calm summer's night and stood in awe at the beauty, the grandeur, the sheer magnificence of what you beheld? I have done so many times, and the desire to reach out and touch the distant canvas of swirling luminaries is still very much alive in my heart. I remember, even as a child of two, being held in my father's arms in a dark forest clearing, looking out into the celestial bliss of light, pointing to the sky and uttering what were probably among some of my earliest words, "Stars . . . stars!" They were so real to me, so bright and lovely. And they seemed so close, I could almost touch them.

Awe, or at least the desire for awe, is something that never completely dies in our hearts, no matter how old we become or how hard we try to erase it from our minds. That is why we are always searching, always looking for something just beyond our reach. That is why, even in a world as dangerous and unpredictable as our own, so many of us have become determined (if somewhat disoriented and restive) pilgrims who, in the face of so much sadness and disillusionment, have pulled in our bellies, tightened our belts, and set out under the darkness of the starry night in search of hope.

A Distant Mirror

The purpose of this book is to rekindle the embers of awe in our hearts so that the wayward pilgrim in each of us can find his or her way more easily in the darkened circumstances of the world we live in. A near-universal human phenomenon, pilgrimage is deeply allied to our desire to transcend the limits of our horizons and to draw back, be it ever so briefly, the dark, unknowing veil of the divine. Down through the centuries, people from all cultures and from all walks of life have left their homes (and often their homelands) to set out on the long, harrowing road of the religious wayfarer. They did so to come close to what they could not touch, to approach the elusive presence of the holy, to be near what they yearned for, to be as close to the stars as they possibly could be.

The roots of pilgrimage go deep in Western culture and had a particularly brilliant flowering in the Middle Ages. At that time, Christians donned the pilgrim's garb for many reasons: to do penance for their own sins or those of others, to gain indulgences, to sell their wares, to swap stories, to meet people from other lands, or simply to see the world. Medieval pilgrims set out for any one of a number of holy and sacred shrines scattered throughout Christendom: Vezelay, Santiago di Compostela, Rome, the Holy Land. Depending on where they started and where they were going, their journey could last weeks, months, even years. Whatever the specifics of each journey, the pilgrim's life was a curious mix of boredom, hardship, drudgery, and determination.

To protect themselves from brigands, thieves, and other wayside hazards, pilgrims normally traveled in groups. The vast array of characters in the "Prologue" of Chaucer's *Canterbury Tales* gives us a good idea of the kinds of people who would set out as a traveling troupe of pilgrims. Together, they would make their way from day to day, from one resting place to the next, in all kinds of weather, and facing many roadside dangers, until they reached their common destination. These loosely knit bands provided food, protection, solace, and friendship for the weary and often homesick travelers. A kind of surrogate "home away from home," these convenient ties proved to be close, but amazingly short-lived. Upon reaching their destination, most pilgrims performed their religious obligations, exchanged farewells, and then quietly disbanded without fanfare or ceremony. The end of their journey heightened for them the transitory nature of all earthly goods as they went their separate ways and embarked upon the next leg of their pilgrimage through life.

The Inward Journey

We live in a very different world from that of our medieval forebears. We have a similar yearning for transcendence, but we find ourselves adrift in a sea of cultural uncertainties that bring into question many of the things our predecessors simply took for granted: the existence of God, the grandeur of creation, natural law, and human nature, to name just a few. Our present world expounds a relativistic view of life at every turn and fills us with both a sense of nostalgia for our simpler, less sophisticated past and an underlying sense of confusion about the meaning of our own life. For this reason (and surely a host of others), our pilgrim's journey has shifted away from the meandering back roads of Christendom and takes place now on the interior footpaths of the soul. There, we encounter hazards just as grave and as dangerous as any wayside danger from here to Canterbury. We also face great uncertainty: we know not what we shall find; we know not if we shall ever arrive; we are not even quite sure just what it is we are looking for.

Ours is one of the first generations for whom the stars have lost their strange, transcendent appeal. No longer do they relate to us the eternal stories of embattled gods; no longer do they elicit from us the inspired dreams of journeying kings; no longer do they move us to our knees in gratitude for the power we have to behold them. We have analyzed them to so great an extent that they have become surprisingly irrelevant in our lives. Their distance from us is too great to bewilder us; their chemical composition, too ordinary to evoke wonder in us. We watch them through our telescopes but have forgotten how to ponder them with our hearts. It is sad to say, but true: the stars do not mean the same for us as they did in former times. They immerse us not in hope, but in an endless sea of uncertainties and force us, almost out of necessity, to turn our gaze elsewhere.

In search of distant stars to call our own, some of us have mustered the courage to look within ourselves. Those of us who have not been intimidated by the initial discomforts have found there a world that is strange and yet familiar: a world as "unimaginably large" but also as "unambiguously finite" as the one our medieval ancestors once traveled.[1] We have even encouraged others to set out with us on a journey of spiritual discovery, although the immensity of the task looms large before us and we ourselves remain hesitant and uncertain about how to proceed. In desperate need of someone to help us to recognize the movement of the stars within our hearts, we long for some wayside traveler to happen along, someone who senses our present disillusionment and deep spiritual hungers and who has already traveled, at least in part, a number of these winding and unfamiliar paths.

A Kindred Spirit

One such person is Vincent Van Gogh (1853–1890), the Dutch post-impressionist of extraordinary artistic genius, whose finely tuned aesthetic sense provides our inchoate desires for transcendence with a vision, however faint, of the stars we once yearned for. An epileptic who suffered from deep bouts of depression, this rising young artist had a thirst for beauty that was perhaps too fragile for the likes of our rough-and-ready workaday world. That works such as *The Starry Night* (1889), *Cypresses* (1889), and *Old Man in Sorrows* (1890) continue to evoke such deep emotions attests to the power of his work.

To find his way through his own looming interior darkness, Van Gogh threw himself headlong into his work. For hours on end, he stood fixed in place, as if in a trance, immersing himself in color and motif, shade and perspective, movement, line, contrast and shape. Again and again, he crossed his brush across the unwilling canvas, seeking to let loose the inner life of what he instinctively felt was just within reach. Time vanished as he created a world where eternity passed with every stroke of the brush and where space was measured by the short distance from the canvas to his heart. Canvas, oils, easel, brush, and palette were the instruments he used to quiet his inner beasts, but his delicate constitution eventually brought on a physical and emotional breakdown from which he would never recover. His health and sanity moved in steady decline. Finally, he could not even pick up a brush without painful headaches and frightening hallucinations.

Van Gogh's art reveals a highly sensitive ear, one that was able to listen to the visible world and allow it to sing its song across the blank space in front of him. Through his oils and pastels, he was able to unite the visible world with the world of his heart. Van Gogh experienced this union within as he painted, but, with his highly refined artist's sense, he also transposed it onto the canvas before his eyes. As a result, his art resounds with a dynamic juxtaposition of countervailing forces: brightness and darkness, movement and stillness, background and foreground all rush together to form an impression of the inner life of the visible world. Intense contemplation enabled him to paint the imprint that the visible world had impressed upon his soul. His humility before nature calmed his own soul and produced in his great moments of creativity something for which generations since have been grateful.

Under the Starry Night

Because of Van Gogh, the starry night of the vaulted sky above has come close and impressed itself upon the solitary canvas of the human heart. His work inspires in those who behold it the same yearning for transcendence that, in previous epochs, drove sinners to their knees and mystics into ecstasy. If the life he led has today become more socially acceptable (a thought he doubtless would have found distasteful), the experience his art conveys remains all the more probing and disconcerting. His canvases disturb our shallow preconceptions of the way life is and reveal for us the uncharted waters of life's primordial sea. They provide a place for nonbelievers to ponder the mystical dimensions of life and for believers to delve beneath the surface of their sacrosanct formulations. They allow people of all walks of life to examine the unexamined and to look again at what they once thought commonplace.

Van Gogh, however, offers more than an aesthetic experience. He challenges us to contemplate the hidden life of the outer world and to find its faint reflection in the inner crevices of the heart. He bids us to cross (be it ever so briefly) our inner threshold of madness and to glory with delirium in the wonder of the present moment. He inspires us to be with our brokenness and to listen to the voices of color, light, and movement as they struggle with our own inner demons. He paints on our souls a vision of a life large enough to live for with passion and die for without regret. He arouses in us a different kind of prayer, one that ponders the dance of the stars above and sees their reflection in the turbulent movements of the heart. He also reveals to us a different sort of God, one whose revelation comes gradually to those who peer beneath the surface of things and who seems driven by a wild and wandering artistic gaze. While there will never be another quite like Van Gogh, something of who he was and what he stood for lives on in each of us. His tragic life still moves us; his artistic vision still inspires us; his inner demons still haunt us. In one way or another, the heart of every modern pilgrim travels in awe under the brilliant, swirling canopy of his starry, starry night.

From Beginning to End

Inspired both by Van Gogh and by the distant mirror held up to us by our medieval forebears, I now invite you, the reader, to don the pilgrim's garb and to set out with me on a long, painstaking journey from the surface of life to the inner yearnings of the heart. Let us set out, aware that hazards are multiplied for those that go it alone, but aware also that the ways of the heart can be traveled only by those who value the presence of solitude and, at times, even loneliness, in their lives. Let us set out, recognizing that the duration of our journey will differ according to the specific needs of each. For some, it may last a very short time, indeed; others may need extended periods of time to digest what I am about to lay before them. No matter. The important thing is that we set out together in search of self-understanding and end our journey with a deeper awareness of life beneath the surface of things.

Even the inexperienced pilgrim will be familiar with the structure by which I have laid out our itinerary. Most pilgrimages, even those of short duration, have: (1) a point of departure, where pilgrims gather, take leave of their loved ones and start out on their journey; and (2) a destination, where they fulfill their religious duties, take leave of their comrades, and begin their return journey home. In between the two, one normally finds (3) a series of wayside stations or resting places. In some cases these are mere watering holes, where travelers shelter themselves from the elements and refresh themselves for a few precious moments of repose; in other cases, they are inns or taverns, where tired pilgrims can strengthen themselves with hot food and spirits, exchange stories from their journey, and bed down for the night. These welcome points of respite provide the nourishment that allows the pilgrim to continue with the next leg of his or her journey.

Integral as they are to the successful completion of the pilgrimage, however, the stopping points are secondary to the actual journey itself. As any pilgrim worth his or her salt will tell you, the most important thing that happens on a pilgrimage occurs nearly always *along the way,* in between the point of departure and the destination, in between even whatever taverns and watering holes they may find along the road. Like the disciples on their way to Emmaus (Lk 24:13–35), the pilgrim's heart burns within as he or she encounters Christ somewhere along the way, nearly always in the most unexpected of places.

In the pages that follow, I offer you a similar arrangement. The journey of the heart upon which we are about to embark has a point of departure and a destination. These are not places, but experiences. I have found that poetry is a helpful way to convey these experiences. Our point of departure, my short poem, "Secret Stars," emphasizes the difficult task before anyone who embarks on the long inward journey to self-understanding. Those inner stars are difficult to discern, easy to overlook. Still, there is something that pushes us onward, that urges us not only to embark on that journey, but also to delve beneath the parts of ourselves that we conceal from ourselves to discover the wonder of who we really are. Our destination, my longer poem entitled, "The Traveler's Rest," speaks of life itself as a journey and brings to consciousness the one point that sometimes even the most veteran pilgrims will forget—that the journey extends beyond our final hour. These two poems seek to express the beginning and the end, the Alpha and the Omega, of our common journey of the heart. You may find it helpful if you keep them in mind.

Just as any pilgrim on the road will, at various points of the journey, look back to his or her point of departure with a nostalgia for friends and family, or forward to his or her destination with anticipated fervor, so I encourage you to look both backward and forward as you make your way through the pages of this book. Only by keeping these two points at least on the periphery of your mind will you be sufficiently prepared to encounter and then digest what lies between them. Only then will you be ready to meet the holy in the most unexpected places.

For your refreshment, I have also included a number of wayside stations (or "legs," as I prefer to call them), where you can listen to the reflections and personal experiences of a fellow traveler and decide for yourself whether or not they warrant more attention for your own spiritual pilgrimage. These are ten prose reflections of various lengths and literary genres, each of which is preceded by a short, introductory poem or story and then followed by a series of "travel questions," specifically designed to help you deal in a more personal way with the material under consideration. Taken as a whole, these legs of our journey cover a wide range of topics and embrace such themes as hope, solitude, searching for lost innocence, confronting failure, the crisis of the heart, conversion, friendship, community, and our image of God. Some of them may appeal to you; others may not. I offer them, not as the final word on the topics they treat, but only as a helpful guide for future reference. Read them as they appear or in whatever order you choose. Read all of them, or only a few of them. Read them in a single sitting, or one per day, or one per week. Tailor this spiritual journey of the heart to your own needs. You are held back only by the limits of your own imagination.

All I ask as you move through each leg of the journey is that you remember your departure point and destination—and that you listen to the stirrings of your own heart. If and when something strikes you, put the book down (it will still be there when you return) and go with the feeling. What is its source and point of origin? Why do you feel the way you do? What is your heart trying to tell you? What are you trying to confront—or trying to avoid? These are the important moments of your journey through this book. Please don't let them slip through your fingers. The travel questions at the end of each chapter

may help you in this regard. Or maybe you will discover
your own way of going about it. Whatever approach you
choose, seize the moment! Examine your secret stars as
you make your way to your traveler's rest. You may not
have the same opportunity again.

Conclusion

So there you have it: we are ready to begin. Come to
think of it, if you have stayed with me this long, we have
already begun! Inspired by the pilgrims who came before
us, moved by a kindred spirit, determined to follow our
own internal promptings of mind and heart, we have already set out on our long and uncertain spiritual journey.
Together let us make our way, one step at a time, not
knowing what we shall find or how we shall find it. That
is how it is and how it should be, at least for the time being. Yearning and racked anticipation have always been
the close, silent companions of the religious wayfarer.
Without them, there would be no joy in discovery, few
spiritual hungers to satisfy, and little reason to ponder the
canopy of stars within us.

But enough has been said by way of introduction. Now
is the time for your final preparations! Take leave of your
loved ones; find food and drink; bring lamp and oil to light
your way. You now need only to find a quiet place. Settle
down in an easy chair; take your shoes off; get an extra pil-
low, if you prefer. Even the heartiest of pilgrims needs
some small creaturely pleasures to help allay the hardships of the journey. Once you have settled in, start out at
a slow, easy pace, one you feel at home with. The road may
seem short, but it takes many turns and rises at times to
tremendous heights. Don't worry about holding us back.
You can't fall too far behind. Besides, we will be waiting
for you at the resting place just ahead. Godspeed and fare
thee well—until we meet again!

Departure

SECRET STARS

I must inside myself concealed

To see if moments trickle down with time,

Articulate a silent task,

Or wander with a whine;

If none exist or from within reply,

Without I stand till ponder fills the sky:

Beneath, above, beyond my reach

Sheer shining stars supply

The yearning of a distant swell,

The wonder of a sigh.

THE DARK SIDE OF HOPE

I could hardly believe my eyes when I saw the name of the shop: THE TRUTH SHOP.

The saleswoman was very polite: What type of truth did I wish to purchase, partial or whole? The whole truth, of course. No deceptions for me, no defense, no rationalizations. I wanted my truth plain and unadulterated. She waved me on to another side of the store.

The salesman there pointed to the price tag. "The price is very high, sir," he said. "What is it?" I asked, determined to get the whole truth, no matter what it cost. "Your security, sir," he answered.

I came away with a heavy heart. I still need the safety of my unquestioned beliefs.

—Anthony de Mello, "The Truth Shop"[1]

A host of questions confronts our pilgrim troupe at the outset of its journey: "What hazards will we encounter along the way?" "What unexpected joys?" "Will we last the entire way?" "What will we find once we get there?" The spiritual nature of our quest adds a number of other pertinent and probing questions: "What kind of truth are we looking for?" "What must we do in order to find it?" "How will we tell the difference between partial and whole truth?" "Who will be our guide?" Questions such as these bring the hardships of pilgrimage to the fore and remind us of the uncertainties we must face at every bend in the road. If we are looking for the whole truth, we have to be ready to feel some discomfort with our present situation as we unmask self-deceptions that influence the way we look at our lives. Such intense and penetrating self-examination never comes easy. It involves a lot of work.

A Look at Augustine

Let me let you in on something. As I was gathering my thoughts for this first leg of our journey, I was halfway tempted to refer to them as, "The Confessions of a Wayward Christian." I balked at the prospect, first of all, because I thought the term "confessions" would invite too close a comparison with that classic work of the same name by the great bishop of Hippo himself, St. Augustine (354–430), someone whose reputation as both a theologian and an autobiographer is a little hard to live up to. And I wouldn't even try. Nor am I about to display my secret sins in all their foundering, uninspiring (and perhaps even boring) details—no, I will leave that discussion for my spiritual director.

In another sense, however, the figure of Augustine looms large in what I would like to share with you at the outset of our journey. You see, Augustine lived in a time when the world as he knew it was crumbling all around him. The Roman Empire, which from the time of the

Caesars had enjoyed unrivaled prominence in the Mediterranean basin and the surrounding territories, had by the middle of the fourth century A.D. overextended itself militarily and, for a host of complicated social, governmental, and economic factors, was now quickly losing its inner cohesiveness. In Augustine's time, the whole show was beginning to unravel; it was crumbling from both within and without, and the fall of the Roman empire, at least as Augustine knew it, seemed all but inevitable. It is no small matter that, in August of 430 A.D. when Augustine lay dying on his bed, the Vandals had already surrounded and were laying siege to the ancient African seaport of Hippo Regius where he had labored for so many years as bishop and pastor of the flock of Christ. Not long after his death, the city would be theirs and its inhabitants left to the mercy of their ruthless pillaging and looting.

Something similar is happening to us today. We, too, hear talk about the "new barbarians" sweeping through the previously untouchable and sacrosanct achievements of modern Western culture. Ominous Vandal-like invaders are said to have crossed the frontiers of our civilized Western world and, even now, to be making their way to our own front doors. Some, in fact, have already arrived. These valueless, secularized pagans are supposedly undermining the very foundations upon which our civilization rested. They sneer at our God, toss away many of our most deeply held truths, ridicule our belief in human dignity and the sacredness of life, and boldly proclaim the right of the individual to determine right from wrong, good from bad, and to do precisely as he or she pleases. These modern barbarians, however, look just like us! They speak the same language, go to the same schools, wear the same clothes and jewelry, have the same hairstyles, read the same books, see the same movies. They are our neighbors, or relatives, our friends or members of our family. These sinister barbarians, it is said, signal the imminent collapse of our present world view and point to the crisis of values becoming increasingly apparent not only in secular life, but in the church itself. The modern world, then, is slowly fading away, crumbling from within, unable to withstand the constant external pressure of contrary subversive forces. In its wake, it will leave nothing but a heap of cultural ruins.

What are we to make of this disturbing description of imminent collapse? Is it a brilliant insight into the present plight of Western culture? A vague, disconcerting warning of things to come? Or just one more feeble and amateurish attempt at interpreting the present in the light of the past? Better to leave such judgments to experts. Whether or not the details of the picture are accurate is a matter I will leave for others to argue over and settle. As far as I am concerned, the analogy limps (sometimes badly). Nevertheless, it seems to have touched a raw nerve in our contemporary Western consciousness. Many today are feeling the cracks of a crumbling world, a way of life that is falling apart at the seams. The sad thing is that we can do nothing about it; we feel lost, set adrift amidst a sea of uncertainties, looking for refuge, first here and then there, in the hope of finding something that will steer us aright and provide for us the stability of former times. Such is the nature of our current pilgrimage through time.

As a man of late antiquity, Augustine was something of a Janus figure, a man whose genius looked back with nostalgia to the achievements of classical Greece and Rome and with uncertain anticipation to what the future would bring. Little did he know that his work would in many ways form the basis of the next thousand years of Western culture. Little did *we* know that, like Augustine, who mourned the passing of classical Rome, many of us today would be lamenting the passing of our modern world and the coming of another, a period of uncertainties, of anxiety, of darkness, and sometimes outright despair.

A World Without a View

In many respects, our present world view has no clear, defining characteristics other than a strong propensity to criticize, tear apart, explode, and otherwise totally deconstruct any proposal that smacks of certitude. All truths, according to our current culture's credo—and it *is* a credo—are historically conditioned, subject to criticism, and ultimately devoid of transhistorical value.

This tendency to tear down and pull apart was a logical outgrowth of the Enlightenment's fascination with the power of human reason. With nothing else to turn its razor-sharp edge on, reason, one might say, began to dismantle itself. In the last century and early part of the present one, philosophers like Marx, Nietzsche, and Freud, the so-called "masters of suspicion," pried open the cracks in reason's foundation and broke through the walls of its otherwise impregnable fortress. In doing so, they heralded the end of the modern era by leaving nothing but a puzzling debris of discontinuities and broken concepts behind. As a result, we live in a world without a view, a world lacking a cohesive vision about the ultimate questions of life and about the way we should conduct ourselves in human society. As a result, most of us make our way through life's uncertainties by rummaging through piles of discarded answers that no longer convince us. The best we feel that we can hope for is to shelter ourselves with whatever partial answers we can forage from among the ruins.

To my mind, one of the best descriptions of our present experience comes from Walter M. Miller's religious science thriller *A Canticle for Leibowitz*. This novel follows the history of an order of monks established shortly after the devastating effects of a world-wide nuclear holocaust. Their culture is a strange combination: old and new, civilized but barbaric, wild yet tame, quite unsure of itself, yet full of new possibilities both for good and for evil. The purpose of this small group of ill-equipped but determined religious enthusiasts is to sift through the rubble of civilization and to try to reassemble and then preserve for future generations the past achievements of the human race. With no sense of the whole to rely on, no master plan or blueprint to guide them, no sense of where they are going or what they are even looking for, their attempts at reconstructing human knowledge are haphazard and often purely random guesses. As the centuries progress, they preserve volumes upon volumes of highly technical scientific information with barely a clue about its meaning. Sad to say, as the monks collect their dusty, indecipherable tomes, the spiral of violence and hatred in their world continues to grow and eventually brings it once again to the verge of a worldwide catastrophe. After receiving a particularly disheartening report about the start of yet another World War, the abbot of the monastery of St. Leibowitz makes a sad comment on the state of a world that, regardless of its state of technological advancement, somehow never seems to change:

> "Where's the truth?" he asked quietly. "What's to be believed? Or does it matter at all? When mass murders have been answered with mass murder, rape with rape, hate with hate, there's no longer much meaning in asking whose ax is bloodier. Evil on evil, piled on evil . . . I feel like saying words I've never even heard. Toad's dung. Hag pus. Gangrene of the soul. Immortal brain-rot. Do you understand me, Brother? And Christ breathed the same carrion air with us; how meek the Majesty of our Almighty God! What an Infinite Sense of Humor—for Him to become one of us!—King of the Universe, nailed on a cross as a Yiddish Schlemiel by the likes of us. They say Lucifer was cast down for refusing to adore the Incarnate Word; the Foul One must totally lack a sense of humor! God of Jacob, God even of Cain! Why do they do it all again?"[2]

We of the twentieth century have experienced the devastating effects of a worldwide spiritual holocaust and are even now trying to pull ourselves up out of the rubble and make sense out of the tainted, ruined spiritual landscape in which we now find ourselves. Auschwitz, Hiroshima, the Killing Fields, Rwanda, Bosnia, Chechnya—the list goes on and on, and probably will continue to do so. Why are we so bent on deconstructing ourselves? Are we suffering from "gangrene of the soul" or some sort of "immortal brain-rot?" "Where's the truth?" "What's to be believed?" Or "does it matter at all?"

Much of the intense anxiety and psychological suffering that many experience in today's Western world comes precisely from this lack of a reference point from which to experience and make one's way through the vicissitudes of life. We all sense that something is missing, something that we once had, but have now lost and cannot seem to find. Nothing fits together anymore. What holds things in place is only a matter of a person's—or a community's—individual opinion, perspective, or taste.

Lost in the Woods

Why have I been spending so much time describing what our slippery, lackluster world "without a view" is like? I do so because whether we like it or not, this world is *our* world; we can ignore it, pretend it doesn't exist, try to mask it or cover it up, but there is one thing we cannot do—get away from it. What's more, this world "without a view" influences us and affects us often in ways we ourselves are not fully aware of. Its lack of perspective penetrates all we do and has become so much a part of the way we look at life that we are often entirely unaware of it. Whether I like it or not, however, I am a man of my times and have the dubious honor of living out my Christian faith within it. Even though I am unhappy about my culture's influence on me, I cannot get away from it any more than I can disavow the air I breathe, the eyes I see with, or the limbs I walk with. The way we view the world—even if it is perspective-less—has that strong an effect on our lives.

In my experience, people deal with this precarious world "without a view" either by adopting a stance of "absolute relativism," where everything becomes a matter of taste or personal opinion, or "relative absolutism," where absolute stances are taken and adhered to precisely as a reaction against the ever shifting winds of uncertainty. In the first, people simply follow the currents of the contemporary world flow and live their lives wherever those shifting trends may take them. In the second, people react against those currents and attempt to determine their own destiny by turning their boats around and paddling upstream. In both cases, the presence and influence of cultural relativism cannot be denied. Each of these approaches must be dealt with and understood in terms of the other and in the context of the historical currents that brought them about.

The result of either approach, the reality that pervades our present situation, is confusion. For many people, life in the present world is like being lost in the woods. I am reminded of an incident from Patricia Hampl's autobiographical journal *Virgin Time*. Off for a walk in the woods one Friday afternoon, she loses her way and has no idea where to turn:

> Suddenly my heart seized up in terror. In a panic, I realized I didn't know which way was out. I had ambled in, wandered any which way. The panic of adrenaline coursed through me, as primitive as if I were a rabbit sniffing a predator. Prickles of fright froze on the back of my neck, ran down my arms.

> I did what I've read that people—foolish people—do lost in the wilderness: started to run. But just as I began to bolt, I remembered that no matter where I was I couldn't be far from the road, from the known

world. Furthermore, the brook was down there. The brook, if need be, could lead me back. But then the feeling of dislocation came back even stronger, crazier. I couldn't tell which way the brook was going, which way was back. And was it the same brook? Maybe it was another thing altogether. The urge to bolt, to run screaming, was intense. I forced myself to stop, sheerly out of the even deeper panic that once I started running I would truly be lost. A heap of bones a hunter finds ten years later. I'd been in the grove only ten minutes, and yet I was grisly with terror, lost in the fairy-tale woods no innocent wayfarer escapes from alive.[3]

The intense anxiety present just below the skin of the modern wayfarer comes from a sense of having lost our way: in life, in our relationships, in our values, even in our faith. We are very good actors and can do very well pretending. We can easily deceive ourselves into thinking that everything is all right, that all will be well. We sense, however, the irate barbarian screaming out inside of us, lost and disoriented, wondering what to believe and which way to turn.

Let's be honest. We have been shaped by and presently live in a culture of uncertainty. To cope with it and, in some cases, simply to survive, we sift through the ruins of our past, hoping to find something that will bring us comfort, something that will give us a sense that, even if we are lost, the road must be somewhere nearby or that the brook will lead us back. Still, we are uncertain. We are afraid. We know not which way to turn. And no matter which way we go, we are not sure if we will find our way home again.

A Restless Spirit

Not long ago, I had the opportunity to travel to St. Rémy-de-Provence in southern France and visit the chapel of the convalescent home where Van Gogh spent a year of his life painting some of his most striking canvases, among them his world-famous *The Starry Night*. He had come to this abbey-turned-sanatorium in a futile attempt to ward off the disquieting shadows that haunted him in both his waking and sleeping hours, and which eventually caused him to take his own life. The space created by the stone walls of the chapel's Romanesque nave has a chilling effect on the heart. It seemed haunted by the spirit of a man whose delicate sense of life's inner beauty was strangely and inexplicably heightened by the tragic circumstances of his waning sanity.

More than a century after his death, we follow in the footsteps of Van Gogh. If the vying voices of his fragmented inner life could not bring him to believe in the God whose passion, death, and resurrection were daily celebrated in the cold, stony nave of the sanatorium chapel, they nonetheless led him to affirm with rare saint-like passion the hidden beauty of the visible world around him. Ever since his youth, he had waged his tragic struggle to articulate his vision of a life beneath the surface of life. This artistic passion cost him many things: his security, his health, his sanity and, finally, his life. If Van Gogh was a man without a traditional faith, his life, his death, his art, and his memory nevertheless remind us of the deep yearning we all have to transcend the limitations which both confine us and make us what we are.

Van Gogh lived in an age when the "masters of suspicion" were already developing the theories that would undermine reason's pronounced self-confidence and set in motion the forces that would bring about the demise of the entire Enlightenment project. Maybe it was his extremely sensitive spirit—a blessing and a curse—that enabled him to reflect in his art the precarious dilemma of an entire century to come. Maybe it was his ability to feel with his brush and to sense in his own heart the hidden turmoil of the world without that enabled him to reveal with canvas and oils the deeply repressed emotions that lurked just beneath the calm, rational veneer of civilized life. Maybe it was his restless spirit which forced him to fly in the face of established convention and to forge his own solitary way of becoming one with the world around him.

Van Gogh the mystic was besieged by powerful inner demons who turned his dreams into nightmares and who slowly gnawed away at his rich inner life. Is it sheer coincidence that many of us feel much the same way? Change a few of the circumstances and Van Gogh's dire story is not all that very different from our own. In his life, we find a faint resemblance to our own troubled yearning for transcendence and inner disquiet among the ruins of reason's tumbled edifice. Even those of us who follow the decaying roads of reason's former glory find the solitary figures of doubt and self-deception as our constant, albeit unwelcome, companions. No profession of faith, however strong, no expression of hope, however great, no admission of love, however deep, can long escape their merciless interrogations. They whisper constantly in our ears and barely give us time to think things through. The results confirm the suspicion that faith in our present age rarely comes without great cost and personal sacrifice. Belief no longer presents itself as a priceless pearl to the inquiring mind. Our age of innocence has come and long since passed. With the Enlightenment now all but a memory, the door through which we have stepped has closed irreversibly behind us. Amidst the ruins which faith must now inhabit, we long for the shelter of former times and tremble at the thought of what the future will bring.

The Man Who Planted Trees

What are we to do in the face of such sad and tenuous circumstances? How can we live in a world where the forces of relativism and pietistic absolutism hold sway over the thoughts we think and the lives we live? What alternative is there to either going with the flow or paddling upstream? I guess it is true that in such trying situations all one can really do is hope. But there are many shades and colors of hope. In the present situation, hope must coexist with doubt and uncertainty, with pain and ambiguity, with the feeling of being lost and with the silent forces of self-deception. Being a Christian in our present world means living on the dark side of hope.

The shepherd in Jean Giono's *The Man Who Planted Trees* is someone who learns to survive and flourish in a life lived on the dark side of hope. He lives in a barren, unsheltered land, where the wind howls across the lifeless terrain and nothing grows under the hot scorching sun. Day after day, month after month, year after year, he traverses the countryside in search of a place for his hungry sheep to graze. During his difficult and, at times, seemingly hopeless labors, he takes the time to carry with him a huge burlap sack of acorns. Wherever he goes in this barren wasteland, he pokes his long iron staff into the ground, and plants his acorns, one at a time, with uncommon care, leaving a trail of seeds in the earth that, he hopes, will reap an abundant harvest in the future. And so it does. Years later, long after the shepherd has died, the countryside is transformed into lavish and beautiful landscape. A passing visitor describes the scene thus:

> Everything was changed. Even the air. Instead of the harsh dry winds that used to attack me, a gentle breeze was blowing, laden with scents. A sound like water came from the mountains: it was the wind in the forest. Most amazing of all, I heard the actual sound of water falling into a pool. I saw that a foundation had been built, that it flowed freely and—what touched me most—that someone had planted a linden beside it, a linden that must have been four years old, already in full leaf, the incontestable symbol of resurrection.[4]

To live on the dark side of hope is to plant the seeds of hope where seemingly nothing is willing to grow. It means traversing the barren lands of despair and isolation that mar the inner landscape of our souls and prevent us from living life to the fullest. It means having a certain stubbornness of heart, a refusal to give in to the seemingly hopeless situations in which we constantly find ourselves. It means going about our task, day after day, month after month, year after year, often without the benefit of seeing with our own eyes the fruits of our labors. The visitor who witnesses that resurrected landscape has some choice words regarding the man who planted trees:

> When I reflect that one man, armed only with his own physical and moral resources, was able to cause this land of Canaan to spring from the wasteland, I am convinced that in spite of everything, humanity is admirable. But when I compute the unfailing greatness of spirit and the tenacity of benevolence that it must have taken to achieve this result, I am taken with an immense respect for that old and unlearned peasant who was able to complete a work worthy of God.[5]

We too are unlearned peasants living in a wasteland of broken certitudes and unknown relativities. We too are foraging for food in an unkind world that often verges on the brink of despair and that has little to offer by way of hope. Am I being too harsh or too pessimistic? Am I emphasizing too much the negative side of life in the postmodern world and not enough of the positive? I think not. This, I believe, is simply the truth about the world we are living in. Facing such darkness is painful. We have to come out from the safety of our unquestioned beliefs—and that is never easy. Let us not forget the well-chosen words of Thomas Merton:

> Only the man who has had to face despair is really convinced that he needs mercy. Those who do not want mercy never seek it. It is better to find God on

the threshold of despair than to risk our lives in a complacency that has never felt the need of forgiveness. A life that is without problems may literally be more hopeless than one that always verges on despair.[6]

Living on the verge of despair and being convinced of our need for forgiveness: such is the never-ending journey of the modern pilgrim. The road before us is long and treacherous.

Venerating Madness

To return to Van Gogh, I had come to St. Rémy with a group of pilgrims, whose faith, by that time, had already been quietly affirmed by visits to more traditional sites of pilgrimage. A visit to St. Bernadette's tomb in Nevers, to St. Margaret Mary's shrine in Paray-le-Monial, or to St. John Vianney's final resting place in Ars transports one back to a simpler, less sophisticated age, to a time when faith and miracles and even the saints themselves could be accepted and gloried in. Van Gogh's place of convalescence evoked a very different set of emotions. Used today as a private retreat for mentally ill women, it put us in touch with the vulnerable side of human existence. There, laughter was upset by sadness; wonder, by painful yearning; joy, by tears of repressed grief. Our emotions ran the gamut of possibility and had a cleansing effect on the soul that few of us had experienced before. And, yet, something else was different. What was it about this place? Why did it seem so strangely familiar? Why did we feel more at home here (of all places!) than in our other points of pilgrimage?

During our visit to St. Rémy, our veneration of sanctity paused momentarily before the living threshold of madness. We came there not to smell the odor of sanctity or to visit saintly remains of incorruptible flesh, but to sniff the natural scent of garden roses and to walk empty hallways that were haunted by the ghost of genius. We came there not to seek a special favor or to venerate someone who had won the crown of victory, but to surface the inner aching of our hearts and to remember one of life's fragile, beautiful, broken ones. We came there not to pray (although pray we did), but to ache over the open wounds of our souls and to find momentary respite from a hectic and, all too often, unkind world. There, at St. Rémy, we came in touch with the madness that haunts the heart of everyone who struggles to peer beneath the appearance of things and to ward off the griping blows of life's inner demons. There, we came in touch with our own difficult struggle to believe and encountered in our fragmented pains the very real need for healing.

The Mass I celebrated that day had a strange, surrealistic quality about it. There we were, pilgrims off the beaten track, looking for healing on a road rarely traveled by searching believers of any prior age. We came there to display our wounds beneath the small chapel's stone barrel vault and to ask the good God to help us find what Van Gogh so desperately sought during his year of residence there. Our prayer there was not of the usual kind: words were few; images, vivid and strong; sentiments, deep and heart-felt. Transformed by doubt, flickering in the shadows of its own uncertainty, our faith shone forth like a dimly lit lantern in a black cavernous cave. This small, hungering flame cast out just enough darkness to insure our next feeble, hesitant steps; it promised little more by way of warmth and comfort, and not even that until it was needed. There, as we prayed, our inner demons awoke from their complacent stupor and tried to divert our attention. Their voices echoed off the stony walls of our hearts and filled our minds with a great cacophony of distracting images and unsettling noise. Only the horror of our open wounds could make them waver. There in this forgotten sanctuary of solitary madness, tears fell in the silence; our hearts grieved, then quaked; we opened our eyes and felt the huge hovering vault of stone above us open out unto the dazzling brightness of the starry night. For the smallest part of a moment, we merged with the space around us and beyond us, eternity brushed across the canvas of our souls—and all was well.

Conclusion

What do you hope for? What helps you to find your way through life's scattered debris of broken dreams and promises? How do you find your way out of the woods and back to the security of the road? Life on the dark side of hope bids us to look beyond the starry night of the soul and to dream of the other side of solitary darkness, where life gives way to death, and death gives way to mystery.

Let me tell you what *I* hope for. The words are not my own, but I have not yet found a better way to express how I feel. They are the words of a fictitious twentieth-century *poverello*, someone who dreamed of what life should be like and who had the courage to follow suit and live his life accordingly. They are the words of a mystic and visionary, of someone who squandered his fortune to help others in need, who embraced the dark side of life in order to experience its brightness, who managed to find joy in the midst of pain, dignity in the stature of the lowly, the gaze of Christ in the face of human misery. What do I hope for? Let the words of Mr. Blue speak for themselves:

> When the day comes that the sky is emptied of stars, and the sun is black, and the distraught winds have only the void for their lament, I am sure that some- where men will be merry together, somewhere good hearts will greet good hearts, and somewhere our dreams of unbroken love and good talk and laughter will have come true. This is a glorious Somewhere, and it is far nearer to us than the stars. There Our Lady talks of children to unknown mothers who taught their many children the love of her single Son.

There Saint Joseph is a man among peasants. There Xavier is home from his wars, and there Suarez and Aquinas have their arguments out. There Thomas More swaps jests with the older Teresa, while the younger Teresa gathers her roses. There Saint George boasts of his conquest of the dragon, and mayhap the Good Thief listens, or mayhap he hears little Saint Francis singing his songs. It is a good place, this Somewhere. It has been called Paradise. It has been called the Tavern at the End of the World. And it has been called Home. It is only Catholicism that would ever allow the like of me to hope someday to be there.[7]

I believe in this Somewhere, this Tavern at the End of the World. My hope in this Somewhere is stronger than the vast uncertainties and hidden relativities and pious absolutes that fill this gloomy world of ours. Just where this hope comes from I do not know; I sense it is not entirely of my own making. To be honest, sometimes it is the only thing that keeps me going. One day I hope to make my way there. There I hope to meet Blue and Van Gogh, the Man who Planted Trees, Merton, Leibowitz, and a host of other people like you and me who will have the opportunity to share the story of their journey through life on the dark side of hope.

A pious dream? A partial truth? A self-deception? Maybe. Maybe not. Nothing is certain on the pilgrim's journey—not even the safety of our unquestioned beliefs. That's part of the anxiety of living in the present world; it is also part of its excitement. To tell you the truth, I can think of no more exciting time to live than now, at the end of the second millennium, and I would not trade places with anyone from any other period or age in all of history—not even Augustine. So let the barbarians come! Let them continue to assail the walls of reason's crumbling edifice. Let them loot its remains and scatter its debris far and wide across the barren spiritual landscape of the world we live in. Let them slip unnoticed into my heart and let them wreak havoc there in my inherited world "without a view." Try as they may, there are some things of mine (and of yours) they simply cannot understand—and thus will not bother with. It is my choice to believe in Paradise, this Somewhere, this Tavern at the End of the World, this place both you and I refer to as Home. As I wait for its coming, I will simply carry on, doing my best—with anyone who wants to help—planting trees.

Travel Questions

1. Do you ever feel that your world is falling apart, unraveling before your very eyes? In what specific areas of your life does this seem to be so? How has that feeling affected the way you live your life?

2. How do your react to the relativistic currents in the world today? Are you an absolute relativist, who goes with the flow and allows it to take you wherever it pleases? Or a relative absolutist, who paddles upstream in an attempt to determine your own destiny? Have you found in your life another option to follow besides either of these two extremes?

3. Which doubts in your life trouble you the most? Do they ever overwhelm you? What ways have you found to cope with them? Are you living your life on the dark or bright side of hope?

4. What do you hope for in life? Does a list of unspoken priorities guide your important decisions in life? To what extent does that list correspond or depart from your conscious beliefs?

5. Do you believe in that Somewhere, that Tavern at the End of the World, that place called Home? If so, to what extent does this belief motivate and enliven your journey through life? What practical relevance does it have for your everyday life? Are you willing to live and die for this belief?

The Second Leg

DESERT
REFLECTIONS

No bright flower blooms, no sweet bird calls,
Nor hermit ever abode,
Not a green thing lifts one lowly leaf,
O God, on the Lonely Road!

—From Seumas Macmanus, "In Dark Hour"[1]

To get to this Somewhere, this Tavern at the End of the World, this place we call Home, involves a long and harrowing journey through the lonely wastelands of the heart. The desert experience is part and parcel of the pilgrim's quest and manifests itself, on the one hand, in a heightened sense of wayfaring through wild and unruly places and, on the other hand, in a feeling of displacement from the ordinary routine of life. We who have set out in search of our Home by the light of the starry night must be ready to traverse similar desert expanses and to face what lies beneath the surface of the ordinary. The two reflections offered on this leg of our journey pertain to these feelings—first, of senseless wandering and second, of intense loneliness—that often accompany us along the way. The first uses the Exodus experience of the Jews as a metaphor for our current spiritual plight; the second recounts an experience of solitude from a recent visit of mine to the Cistercian abbey of Sénanque.

A Life of Wandering

The sands of the desert stretch before our eyes, reminding us of the dry, sterile dust from which we have come and to which we shall return. Hunger and thirst accompany us during our somber sojourn through life. The persistent lack of direction in our lives confronts us with the dire need for change. We recognize our spiritual impoverishment, but are unable to do anything about it. The story is always the same. One day leads to the next. Our resolutions weaken. We lose track of time. We fail. Soon, we have lost our way altogether. Will this leg of our journey be any different? Who will lead us out of our confusion? What are the signs that will show us the way out of the barren waste that surrounds us? Sooner or later, there must come a time for pondering such questions about the experience of desert in our lives.

The forty-year sojourn of the Jews in the Sinai desert presents us with a fitting metaphor for our own spiritual plight. Their flight from slavery gave rise to an ongoing drama of life and death in the most desolate of earthly habitats. Led by the groan of their stomachs and the muttering of useless complaints, the Israelites moved from place to place without purpose or direction. From the wilderness of Shur (Ex 15:22) to the wilderness of Sin (Ex 16:1) to the wilderness of Sinai (Ex 19:1), their wandering confounded and confused them. Much worse, it enervated their devotion and weakened their loyalties to God. As they made their journey, the desert winds shaped the contours of their souls; vast was their loneliness and isolation. Murmuring accompanied them both day and night. They felt abandoned by all but their closest companions—hunger and thirst. Signs were in abundance, to be sure: the springs of Elim (Ex 1:27), the provision of quail and manna (Ex 16:13-15), the water from the rock (Ex 17:6-7), the theophany at Sinai, and the making of the Covenant (Ex 19-20). God had not and would not abandon them. But they abandoned God. Time and time again, they would draw up their own plans and go their own way. Wandering had become a way of life for them, and it took the initiative of God to bring them to their senses.

Like the Israelites of old, we too have grown accustomed to a life of wandering. Our deserts, however, are works of human hands rather than those of nature. Walls of concrete, not shifting sands, provide the scenery for those who sojourn there. Herded together in anonymous city dwellings, we move as a crowd through a continuous maze of passing fads. We have surrounded ourselves with the latest conveniences of life, but shudder with fright from an aching inner loneliness. Groaning and complaint permeate the air we breathe. We are driven by hungers and thirsts for things which gnaw at our spirits: *pleasure, power,* and *possession.* Temptations abound, but we cannot

overcome them. We are lost in the desert and not even
aware of it. One place is as good as the next; one day, the
same as another in the wasteland of the human heart.

God in the Desert

Wherever we go, God has gone before us—even in the
desert. This was lesson repeated for the Israelites by myriad signs and wonders. Unfortunately, it was a hard lesson
for them to learn. Signs alone cannot sustain a journey in
faith: People are impressed by them at first, but once their
absence is felt, as eventually happens, life soon reverts to
normal. For the Israelites, then, their desert pilgrimage became a life of "wandering between the signs."

Their conversion was a result not of their own doing,
but of God's dogged persistence to carry them along. His
dream of them as his chosen people and his refusal to give
it up eventually got through to them. The Covenant of
Sinai grew out of Yahweh's continuous wandering with his
people. During that time, the Jews were slowly turned by
God from a loosely bound group of bedouin tribes into a
closely knit and deeply religious people. Their momentary
glimpses of his majesty taught them to trust in his power
to overcome all obstacles, physical as well as spiritual. With
Yahweh as their Lord, they had nothing to fear. He would
eventually lead them to the land of promise.

God will also lead us through the wilderness of the human heart. He has, in fact, already gone there to prepare
our way. After his baptism by John in the Jordan, Jesus "was
led into the desert by the Spirit" (Mt 4:1). After a fast of
forty days and forty nights, he was harassed by those urges
which have plagued the human heart since the sin of human origins. He was first tempted to turn stones to bread
to satisfy his hunger and thus give himself *pleasure*. His response: "Not by bread alone is man to live" (Mt 4:4). Then,
he was challenged to throw himself off the parapet of the
temple unto the protection of the angels as a display of

power. His response: "You shall not put the Lord your God to the test" (Mt 4:7). Finally, he was directed to pay homage to evil as a condition for receiving all the kingdoms of the world in his *possession.* His response: "Scripture has it: You shall do homage to the Lord your God alone" (Mt 4:10). The episode concludes with the devil giving up and leaving him in peace: ". . . and angels came and waited on him" (Mt 4:11). *Pleasure, power, possession*: Jesus himself encountered the darkness of evil that lurks beneath the surface of the human heart—and he survived! His forty day and nights in the wilderness were but a prelude to his struggle to overcome the ruling passions of the soul.

Wherever and however we journey, God prepares our way. Jesus himself has entered the wilderness of the human heart and has overcome its bondage to the powers of darkness. In baptism, we too are led by the Spirit and follow Jesus into the desert of human passion. With him before us, there is no need to be afraid.

Austerity of Space

Not long ago, I found my way to the isolated, rocky gorge in the southern French region of Provence where there stands, hauntingly well-preserved, one of the purest extant examples of twelfth-century monastic architecture, the great Cistercian abbey of Sénanque. Built in 1148, the abbey was a part of the reform of Benedictine monasticism that emanated from the spiritual powerhouse of Cîteaux in French Burgundy and which was promulgated by so prominent a spokesman as St. Bernard of Clairvaux (1090–1153). The stone walls of this abbey rise from the earth in rugged simplicity and present a heart-rending picture of austerity that is surpassed only by the steep incline of the forbidding limestone hills that surround it. Any visitor to this monastery will find it difficult to escape an encounter with the interior regions of his or her soul. Within its walls, space and time themselves are carefully molded and landscaped to carry the soul into an absorbing and distractionless confrontation with the eternal.

Upon entering the monastery confines, I found myself almost instinctively making my way in silence through its long empty halls and prayerful cloister walk. Sénanque is not a place for the spoken word. Its bare stone walls and towering barrel vaults draw the quiet out of the soul into the surrounding space. My walk through the dormitory and chapter room, through the monks' warming-room and cloister walk made me deeply conscious of the barren solitude around me—and also within me. The abbey seems to have been carved out of the desolate space of the valley it inhabits. In that space, where from dawn to dusk shadows dance with the rhythmic movement of the sun, one encounters the inner movements of shadow and light that both illuminate and darken the vast interior reaches of the soul.

Sénanque is a symbol of the desert experience. Just as its monks came to that desolate wasteland in lower Provence to settle the land and to cultivate its vast resources, so too they used the carefully planned expanse of space within its walls to turn over the soil of the soul and to grow there the fruits of contemplation. At Sénanque, the desert of one's soul opens out onto the desert of the monastery's inner space, which in turn opens out onto the barren wilderness beyond its walls. Like the desert fathers of old, the Cistercian monks who lived, worked, and died there, came to the desert to find God and to save their souls. The struggle was one of survival. All of their energy—all of their hearts, their minds, and their strength—was focused on that one, all-consuming end. There was no room for distraction, for luxury, or for extravagance of any kind. Everything was aesthetically functional: straight lines, plain barrel vaults, little if anything by way of ornamentation or decor. Nothing could be present that would divert their senses, minds or hearts from their long, spiritual quest.

The abbey's austerity of space forces one to look inward and confront oneself beneath the distracting superfluities that clutter the inner corridors of the soul. Its barren stone walls bid us to take off the masks of self-deception that we wear through so much of our journey and to bare our souls to God. Of all the places in the abbey that encourage this deep, inner purging, it is the chapel, with it towering Romanesque nave and transept, that brings us furthest along this difficult and rarely traveled road. There, heaven and earth meet as the pointed barrel vault opens out onto the space of the semi-circular sanctuary. There, beneath the three windows that illuminate the altar and chancel, silence conducts the rising chants of the heart to swell with our innermost yearnings. There, the soul has the chance to be still without being self-conscious and to be itself without wondering about what role to play or what witty word or phrase to express next. There, God is given the space and the time to penetrate our lives with a lasting assurance of deep, endearing love.

Time for the Eternal

A walk through the ancient abbey even immerses one in a different sense of time. There, *kairos* displaces *chronos* as one gradually becomes more attuned to the present moment. One forgets about the clock as seconds and minutes, hours and days, weeks and seasons move without rush or race, each at its own proper pace. Time is not divided by the stroke of the hour or by the tick of a clock, but by the recitation of the psalms and the order of the day. Life seems filled with a sense of the eternal. And the eternal is only as far away, only as elusive, as the abbey's enveloping silence.

The monks at Sénanque sought to sanctify the day through manual labor, liturgy, and spiritual reading. There was a time and a place for everything under the sun: (1) a time for work in the isolated desert spaces beyond the monastery walls, where the Cistercians did wonders transforming the inner spaces of Europe from swamplands into lush farmlands and garden reserves; (2) a time for common liturgical prayer, where the Cistercians gathered in chapel seven times throughout the day and even into the night to sing praise to the glory of God; and (3) a time for private spiritual reading, where each monk spent hours reading and digesting the wisdom of the fathers of the church and Christian monasticism in order to fortify his soul with sound spiritual nourishment. Three different times; three different spaces; three different activities. When followed to the letter (as the Cistercians prided themselves in doing) the Rule of Benedict showed remarkable foresight in its ability to sanctify the various times and places that marked the routine of daily monastic practice.

It also showed an uncanny appreciation of the needs of the whole person. Physical labor exercised the muscles of the body; chanting the psalms nurtured the spirit; spiritual reading increased the monk's mental prowess and provided food for spiritual growth. Body, soul, and spirit: all three dimensions of human existence were taken account of in the normal routine of daily living. The fact that all of these things were done in a communal setting also highlighted the social aspect of the human person. The monk understood himself and his vocation only in the context of his community life. His monastic community was, for him, the school of Christian virtue. It was there where time for the eternal manifested itself in the bonds of spiritual friendship and the exercise of Christian charity.

If Walls Could Talk

After an hour of my silent walk through the abbey's enclosed quarters, my thoughts quietly turned to the huge stone walls of their chapel, then to those of their common dormitory and refectory, and finally to their warming-room and chapter hall. The plain, barren face of these neatly-measured and precisely-sculpted stones stared back at me as I pondered their role in the life of the community. Protection from the elements was only the beginning of what they offered the monks. They also provided them with places in which to pray and to study, to examine their lives and to confess their sins, to nourish their bodies and to give rest to their bones, to recover from sickness, to live and to die. The monks of Sénanque lived out the drama of their lives within these very rooms. If only these stones could talk! I wonder what we would hear?

How many psalms, for example, did they hear from the strong male voices filling the chapel in their daily chanting of the office? How many meals did they watch the monks eat in silence or to the careful meditative reading of Cassian's *Conferences*? How many cold, chilly evenings did they witness the monks gather in the warming-room (the one heated room in the entire monastery) in order to heat their bodies and warm their souls around the fireplace before turning to their straw mats for the night? How many groans did they hear as the monks rose from sleep in the middle of the cold night in order to pray the Night Office? How many faults did they hear confessed as the community gathered in the chapter room to study the rule and then to accuse themselves of infractions? How many penances did they see performed? How many disheartened monks did they see leaving the abbey in order to return to the world beyond the valley? And how many young aspirants did they discover, knocking at the door in search of sanctity in such a distant and isolated part of God's creation? If only these walls could talk! The tales they would recount would undoubtedly fill tomes, the details of which would not be recorded in official registers.

And yet, there is something about Sénanque that even its walls would not be able to reveal. Its buildings exist not for themselves, or for the aesthetic experience they convey, or for what they teach us about an important period of our medieval past, but for one simple purpose: the determined and dogged pursuit of holiness. The abbey's fields and grounds, its quiet cloister walk, its wonderfully molded spaces and splendid architecture, were created as a part of that unrelenting pursuit of sanctity which motivated the Cistercians to lay down their roots in this isolated and desolate valley. The history of this pursuit, however, cannot be recorded in full by the naked eye or by what any stone wall could relate if it could but speak. Such a story must have access to the inner movements and quiet promptings of the human heart. And for this very reason, the full story of Sénanque can only be recorded by the monks who lived, prayed, worked, and died there.

Conclusion

None of what I have said until now could keep me from feeling a sense of sadness as I finished my walk and left the abbey grounds. The glory of Sénanque has long since passed. Its buildings still stand, but something is missing. Although a few monks still live on the premises in appropriately secluded quarters off the square stone cloister, the abbey of Sénanque is not the vibrant monastic center it once was. Today, its main buildings serve as a Cultural Encounter Center where interested people, like myself, can walk through the ancient rooms, learn a little about twelfth-century building techniques, and imagine what life might have been like for those who inhabited these rooms so long, long ago. The buildings are being put to good use, but they are not being used for what they were originally intended. Or are they?

When entering the abbey today, one encounters *more* than just a dusty museum piece of a bygone epoch of Western civilization. Although its fiery blaze has long since subsided, a faint flame still flickers in the long empty spaces which once gave shelter to such a burning and dedicated spiritual quest. Even today, the abbey of Sénanque is sacred ground. How and why can this be so? Because generations upon generations of monks have hallowed its rooms with their desire for holiness; because the ideal of this pursuit is built into the spaces created by this particular type of monastic architecture; because the resulting quiet still draws one out of oneself into the austere, haunting interior spaces within its walls. Even though the sanctuary lamp no longer glows and the smell of incense has long since faded from the air, even though the chapel no longer resounds with the calming, tranquil sounds of Gregorian chant, one cannot help but sense an aura of holiness about the place. This reverence for God and for life is built into very fabric of the monastery. The stones themselves give witness to the glory of God and the goodness of his creation.

A visit to Sénanque awakens the desire for holiness in every heart which takes the time to ponder its deep transfixing spaces, to listen to its walls, and to walk in its chapel and cloister with an open mind and heart. Even today, it beckons the heart to listen to its deepest yearnings and to find there, in the midst of its own land of desolation, the inner voice of God. Sénanque refreshes the soul by transporting it out of the ordinary run of the mill concerns of daily life and by inviting it to open itself up to a deeper dimension of human existence. It bestows the hope on those who come there that contemplation is within their grasp, even when they conclude their visit and carry on with their lives beyond the cloister walls. Such, at least, was the effect that my short stay there had on me. When I left Sénanque that day, I felt as though I had carried a part of it away, within me. I go there often, even now, in the deep interior and desolate regions of my heart, to find a quiet place where I can commune with God, give rest to my weary soul, and leave refreshed, ready to go on with my journey.

Travel Questions

1. What have been the desert experiences in your life? How did you survive them? Would you go through

them again if you had to? What would you have done differently?

2. Think back to a particular moment in your life when you felt as though you were wandering without purpose or direction. Try to remember the cause(s) of your disorientation. Did the feeling of abandonment by family or friends have anything to do with it? Where do you think God was in all of it?

3. Have you ever felt as though God were giving you a sign? What precisely was it? A particular event? A thought that crossed your mind? A book you read? The words of a friend? How did you feel at that moment? How did you determine whether the sign was genuine or false?

4. Think of a time when you were especially lonely. Who or what were you longing for? What did you do to get through it? Have you learned to live with and befriend your loneliness? Have there ever been moments in your life when your loneliness has been transformed into solitude?

5. Do you have a private space within your heart where you can go to replenish your spirit? What is it like? How do you get in touch with it? How often do you go there? Have you ever shared this very personal part of your life with another? If not, why not?

The Third Leg

SEARCHING FOR INNOCENCE

"Father! father! where are you going?
O do not walk so fast.
Speak, father, speak to your little boy,
Or else I shall be lost."
The night was dark, no father was there;
The child was wet with dew;
The mire was deep, & the child did weep,
And away the vapour flew.

—William Blake, "The Little Boy Lost"[1]

The desert has a purifying effect on the soul. To survive its rough terrain and scorching heat, the pilgrim must learn to make due, to be content with the bare necessities of life: food, drink, adequate clothing and footwear—nothing more, nothing less. The demands of the journey teach him or her not to burden the back with superfluous luxuries that can all too easily slow one down and even hinder one's progress along the way. Of necessity, the pilgrim walks a way of simplicity. The traditional garb donned by a medieval pilgrim— a broad-rimmed hat, a woolen cloak, a traveling staff and haversack—symbolizes in outward form the interior purging that his or her journey is to have on the soul. For the modern pilgrim, this path of simplicity manifests itself in the search for innocence. Those of us who seek it desire to experience again the wonder of life through the eyes of a child. Conscious of the paradise we have lost, we try to get in touch with the little child who each of us once was and, to a large extent, still remains. Yearning for attention and for a chance to speak, our inner child kindles in us a renewed hope for finding our way back to the God. The reflection on this leg of our journey focuses on this need for inner simplicity and purity of heart.

A Youthful Memory

At the end of my sophomore year of college, I took a summer job at the Willowbrook Mental Health Facility in Staten Island, New York. I was one of 300 temporary workers brought in by the State of New York to help alleviate the disgraceful conditions that had been unearthed by an FBI investigation and the no-nonsense reporting of a young street-wise television reporter for Eyewitness News. I knew from the start that I was nothing but a drop in the bucket, that such stopgap measures were like putting a Band-Aid on a bleeding artery. I knew there was little that I or any of my young coworkers could do to change the situation. I also knew that my job was more a political response to public outrage than an honest attempt to make things better for the patients. Despite these hard practical realities, I jumped at the chance of being on the state's payroll. A job was a job, I thought. Heavily in debt because of my college loans, I was grateful to be duly employed for the months of July and August.

No prior experience in my life had prepared me for what I was to experience firsthand at Willowbrook. "The kids," as we called the patients there, were nearly all severely mentally disabled and, to my mind, treated like animals. More than twenty years later, I can still vividly recall how some of them were needlessly over-medicated by well-meaning but ill-prepared nurses, who could barely read their names off their identification bracelets; stitched up by inconsiderate physicians, who preferred to tolerate their screaming rather than administer a light, inexpensive anesthetic; and put to bed by unfeeling attendants who, when supplies ran low, saw nothing strange in depriving them of pajamas, sheets, or pillowcases for the night.

A Lasting Impression

The aggressive indifference of many on the permanent staff made matters even worse. One day I saw a small group of them laughing at Frankie, one of our "thirty-year-old two-year-olds" (as we liked to call them), whose large forehead and protruding brow gave him an uncanny resemblance to Boris Karloff. As I got closer, I saw that Frankie was happily chewing on something with his customarily wide, childlike grin. As I drew within arm's reach, I noticed the brownish color of his teeth and realized that the unmistakable smell could only be one thing.

"Go ahead, Frankie, eat some more! There's plenty more where that came from!" Some of the staff members could not contain their laughter: "Hey Frankie, is that what they feed you at home? Why don't you go back and ask for more!" When I realized what was happening, I grew disgusted with them for their open callousness toward someone under their charge and then with myself for being too afraid to confront them (I had already been threatened once for interfering in the way things were run around there). As I wiped out his mouth with my handkerchief and took him to the shower room to clean out the rest of it with soap and water, I remember thinking to myself, "Is this what we've come to?" "What kind of a warped, bent-out-of-shape place *is* this?"

The memory of this particular incident haunts me to this day. Never before had I come so close up against the reality of humanity's inhumanity. Never before had I felt so helpless in the face of such blatant human degradation. Never before had I experienced what cold, premeditated indifference could do to the dignity of another individual. Frankie was one of God's innocent ones. He could hardly walk, barely talk, and would not hurt another soul even if he knew how. He did not ask to be born the way he was. How could anyone be so cruel and thoughtless as to ridicule someone who did not even know how to argue back or defend himself?

My anger that day was pointed in many directions: at the staff workers for their utter insensitivity to another human being (and, worse yet, to someone under their care); at myself, for giving in to my fears of being threatened, ostracized, or physically hurt; at the State of New York for allowing the conditions at Willowbrook to degenerate to such a point; and even at God for permitting such actions under his vast omnipresent gaze. There was no way I could be angry at Frankie; he did not even know what he was doing and would have been perfectly content if I had allowed him to continue eating his own waste. Despite his disgusting treatment, his childlike demeanor brings to mind the calming, hopeful words of Jesus: "Let the children come to me . . . It is to just such as these that the kingdom of God belongs" (Mk 10:14).

Our Human Handicap

Over the years, I have discovered my own potential for cruel and insensitive behavior. I myself have been indifferent to the plight of other people, sometimes even to the point of ridiculing them. Perhaps the instances were not as dramatic as the one I have just related, but they are nonetheless real and, to my mind, inexcusable. "Bent creatures are full of fears," says the archangel Oyarsa in C.S. Lewis' *Out of the Silent Planet.*[2] I myself am full of them and subject to them in many areas of my life. If such an admission seems to others to be out of sync with the rest of my character, it is only because I have perfected the art of keeping them to myself, locked up in an inner, secret life of my own making.

In his popular bestseller *Maybe (Maybe Not)*, Robert Fulghum writes about this secret life that characterizes so much of the feisty melodrama of human existence:

> Public lives are lived out on the job and in the marketplace, where certain rules, conventions, laws, and social customs keep most of us in line. Private lives are lived out in the presence of family, friends, and neighbors who must be considered and respected, even though the rules and proscriptions are looser than what's allowed in public. But in our secret lives, inside our own heads, almost anything goes.[3]

The *secret* part of our lives normally comprises a messy and unpredictable mixture of both good and bad: "MTV, X-rated video, CD-ROM, and the *National Enquirer* combined couldn't compete with what goes on behind the closed door of the secret side of our minds."[4] There, in those private, intimate quarters, we give birth to the fantasies, dreams, and illusions that accompany us throughout our sleeping and waking hours. There, we delve beneath the rational veneer of human respectability and see the embarrassing—and, at times, surprising—truth about ourselves. There, we carry on a lifelong inner dialogue with our alter ego, that "other self" within us who questions everything we do in our private and public lives and tempts us constantly to throw all discretion to the wind.

Sometimes our secret lives are so secret that even *we* don't know what's going on. The underground currents of the unconscious rise to the surface of our conscious lives and influence our actions in ways we do not fully understand. For better or worse, these hidden elements often spill into and affect the private and public sectors of life. The incident with Frankie was one such example: secret ridicule vented itself publicly; advantage was taken of another's weaknesses; prejudices were voiced and then met with applause. Frankie was thought of and then treated as a freak. In the eyes of those who laughed at him, he was less than human and therefore not worthy of respect. All this and the workers seemed not even aware of what they were doing! Their secret aversion toward Frankie's handicap manifested itself in an unconscionable attack on his human dignity. If hell is "not to love anymore,"[5] as the priest in George Bernanos' novel *The Diary of a Country Priest* suggests, then I have to wonder when I think of these people (and others like them—myself included) who really *was* suffering from a handicap at the time. In the eyes of God, surely not Frankie.

False Self/True Self

How do we deal with this handicap of callousness and insensitivity to the needs of others? How do we overcome our tendency to promote ourselves at the expense of others? What can we do to eliminate the fears that bind us to ways of acting that are fundamentally opposed to the good of others? The answers to such questions are difficult to find and, once found, often hard to accept. They ultimately turn on our inability to change ourselves without the help of God. To humbly accept our limitations and to recognize where our human capacities end and where the power of God takes over is the all-important first step of our spiritual journey. Without it, we are doomed to repeat the same mistakes with all the other helpless misfits we encounter in our lives.

"If I allow myself to degenerate into the being I am imagined to be by other men, God will have to say to me, 'I know you not!'"[6] These words of Thomas Merton demonstrate the importance of our getting in touch with our deepest selves and not living our lives entirely according to the expectations of others. If we truly wish to know and to be known by God, then we must first seek to know and to understand ourselves as we really are:

> We must accept the fact that we are not what we would like to be. We must cast off our false, exterior self like the cheap and showy garment that it is. We must find our real self, in all its elemental poverty but also in its great and very simple dignity: created to be a child of God, and capable of loving with something of God's own sincerity and His unselfishness.[7]

Casting off the false, exterior self means sifting through our public, private and secret lives and keeping only those elements which help us to become more fully human. It means looking at all of these areas of our lives and putting aside those thoughts, attitudes, and behaviors that tear down and consistently get in the way of our capacity to love. It means looking to God for help in rooting out all the fears, aggressive indifference, and outright hatred that keeps us from loving those with whom we journey and which keep us from knowing our deepest, truest selves. Most of all, it means getting in touch with and caring for the frightened little child who wanders around inside each of us. Like Frankie, we are all little children in adult bodies. Unlike Frankie, most of us have accrued highly refined, sophisticated means of self-deception to convince us otherwise.

Searching for Gump

Preserving a sense of childlike innocence even in our adult lives is one of the central themes of the recent box office sensation *Forrest Gump* (1994). The film follows the life of a simpleminded young man, whose substandard IQ works to his advantage by keeping him free of the jaded compromises that normally make their way into our adult lives. A grown man with the mind of a child, Gump accepts people as they are without prejudging them and sees the good in them even when they do him harm. The film traces one episode after another in his unusually eventful and colorful life where, because of his slowness of mind and childlike demeanor, he rises to the occasion and is able to bring out the best in himself and in other people.

"Mama always said, 'Stupid *is* as stupid *does.*'" This pithy aphorism from Gump's early childhood (repeated time and again throughout the film) causes us first to smile at his unassuming naiveté and then cringe at the utterly literal way in which it influences his life. When read in light of his actions, however, it reflects the roots of an ancient wisdom that we have all but forgotten in our strident march toward the technological advancement of our race. *Being* has much to do with *doing*—and vice versa.

To change our character for the better we must develop healthy habits of behavior that become, in time, a second nature to us, a part of who and what we are. Despite his mental limitations, Gump grasps this all-but-forgotten principle of life and makes it so much a part of himself that, even when events take an unexpected turn for the worse, he finds the resources within himself to do what is right. Gump's way of speaking about life may appear shallow and off the point to more sophisticated eyes. Let us not, however, be quick to judge. Perhaps it is we who have lost the power to penetrate the deep-down truth of things.

The movie's strong moral content is one of the reasons why it has captured the imagination of moviegoers across the world. Said to be a fable based on the *Tao Te Ching* (The Way of Life), by Lao-tzu, it highlights those qualities of the fool that should be held in high regard by all people, young or old, rich or poor, black or white, male or female:

> These possessions of a simpleton being
> the three I choose
> And cherish:
> To care,
> To be fair,
> To be humble.
> When a man cares he is unafraid
> When he is fair he leaves enough for others,
> When he is humble he can grow. . . . [8]

Gump's actions reflect these values throughout the movie and reveal to us the kind of man he is. Because he cares, he overcomes his fear of death and heroically saves the remainder of his ambushed squad in the jungles of Vietnam. Because he is fair, he freely shares the good fortunes of his successful shrimping venture with anyone who comes to him in need. Because he is humble, he allows Jenny, his childhood sweetheart, to blaze her own trail through life, but is there in her moment of need when she has no one else to turn to. On every point, Gump comes across as a man of great love and compassion. His utter simplicity and lack of guile allow him to be a man for others, someone whose handicap is really a gift and something to be admired.

However one interprets the film—as a philosophical commentary on the virtuous life, a fable of Taoist wisdom, or even a Christian parable about the seductive nature of knowledge and humanity's deep longing to return to its unfallen, pristine state—it attracts people because they find something of themselves reflected in Gump's childlike innocence. All of us yearn to meet the little child who wanders alone within our adult hearts and who, for whatever reason, has been locked away in our hidden, secret lives and rarely, if ever, allowed to go outside and play. When viewed in this way, the film invites us to let down some of the inhibiting and restrictive barriers in our lives that prevent us from being our deepest, truest selves.

Observations

The examples of Frankie and Gump have much to tell us about the way we live our lives and the type of people we are called to become. Five points in particular stand out.

1. The way we react to others is often a reflection of what is going on within us. If we ever lose touch with the child we once were and, to a large extent, still are, we will forget how to look at life with the sense of innocence, mystery, and wonder that characterizes so much of our early years. Once this happens, our relations with others can become merely functional, and it will be all too easy to treat them with less respect than they deserve. Frankie and Gump remind us of the importance of nurturing and caring for the inner child in each of us. If we do not, we may find ourselves contributing to rather than lessening the unwieldy spiral of hatred and aggressive indifference in the world around us.

2. If actions in the outer world do reflect those in the inner world, then it makes perfect sense for us to try to be sensitive to the interior state of those we deal with. When we see through the smoke screen of others' external actions and sense the real needs that are locked up in their secret lives, we are able to delve beneath the surface of life and understand the reasons for the way they act. Being aware of another person's neglected inner child and tending to its needs helps to free us from the fears and learned attitudes that have caused us to act in a bent manner towards others. Healing another's inner life can do much to effect a change in his or her external behavior.

3. The fear of being thought "stupid" puts us on guard and influences much of our external behavior. Because it has so often confused knowledge with wisdom, Western culture presently finds itself adrift in a sea of unprecedented technological progress without any stable, viable means of evaluating it. As Gump teaches us, wisdom means caring, sharing, and growing with others. It is not so much a matter of raw intelligence as an attitude toward life that enables us to embrace it with wonder and awe. Gump, and, to a lesser extent Frankie, teach us that too much knowledge may not be such a good thing, that sometimes it is necessary to have less of a good thing in order to appreciate its place in the whole. They teach us that the fear of being thought stupid is rooted in our own inability to accept our natural limitations and of our desire to be something other than what God made us to be.

4. Nurturing our neglected inner child is another way of talking about the call to conversion. Like any analogy or metaphor, it has its limitations and needs to be complemented by other, equally valid approaches. Such an insight, however, should not lead us to underestimate what nurturing the inner child can do to help us. While there is a very real danger of becoming overly introverted and focused on unfulfilled childhood needs, its role as a powerful metaphor to help us to integrate our early life experiences with our psychological and spiritual well-being cannot be easily discounted. Searching for Gump means becoming the person each of us is meant to become. Its strengths far outweigh its weaknesses as a way of talking about the need for conversion in our lives.

5. Finally, searching for, finding, and nurturing our inner child cannot be done apart from God's help. "Let the children come to me and do not hinder them. It is to just such as these that the kingdom of God belongs" (Mk 10:14). Allowing the neglected child within us to come out from its

hiding place and to trust us—we who have spent so much time scolding it, repressing it, and otherwise downright ignoring it—will not take place unless the child itself somehow senses the presence of Jesus calling and promising that everything will be okay. If the kingdom of God truly is within us, then it must surely belong to the neglected child within each of us. The healing of that child is first and foremost the work of God. All we can do is pray (itself a gift) and share in the work that God promises to do in our lives.

Conclusion

We share a lot in common with all the Frankies and Gumps who inhabit this strange world of ours. Neglected and ostracized because of their handicaps, they remind us of our yearning to return to life's primordial garden and evoke from us a sense of what we once were and what, with God's grace, we can still become. They elicit a sense of our own human frailty and make us wonder what life would be like if the circumstances were different and we suddenly found ourselves in their shoes. Most of all, they teach us about the cost of living innocently in a world that wallows in suspicion and so often prefers to pull down for the sake of pulling down.

Although it happened so long, long ago, my summer at Willowbrook is still very fresh in my mind. The incident with Frankie is only one of many stories that I can recount as if they happened yesterday, so deep was the impression they made on me. Willowbrook, I now realize, had become the social waste bin of New York State. As an institution, it had perfected the art of giving care without care and succeeded in dehumanizing not only the patients who lived there, but even the people who worked there. Strangely enough, I count my time there as one of the most formative periods of my life. It made me realize how far we will go out of our way *not* to help another person in need. It made me realize for the first time in my life how cruel one human being can be to another. And it forced me to come to terms with my own biases and prejudices, especially those just beneath the surface of my skin.

As luck (or Providence) would have it, Willowbrook closed a long time ago as a mental health facility of the State of New York. Allowed to remain vacant and out of use for a few years (a necessary penance, perhaps, after the perpetuating so horrible a social evil), its buildings presently form a part of the newly renovated campus of the College of Staten Island, one of the current show pieces of the New York City University system. Aside from the occasional wisecrack about the college "taking the place" of Willowbrook, the arrangement is a good one and has had a very positive effect on the local community. When I pass it on the road, however, I sometimes think to myself, "If walls could talk, the students at this college would get a lesson they'd never forget." On one occasion, I even mustered the courage to go to the building where I once worked. Unwilling to enter, I hung about on the outside, poking my head here and there, looking, almost instinctively, for Frankie's familiar grin and whatever Gump-like figure might happen along. I sighed with relief when neither crossed my gaze. I also smiled with hesitant recognition when I realized, for the first time in my life, that they *were* there—lurking somewhere within my own hidden, secret life—begging for attention.

Travel Questions

1. Have you ever seen someone gravely mistreating another person? What did you do (or not do) about it? What would you have done differently if you could? Have you yourself ever received grave harm from another? How did the victim in you respond?

2. In what way has "our human handicap" manifested itself in your life? Have you ever felt overwhelmed by the darker side of yourself? How has it shown itself in your relations with others? How have you learned to live with it ?

3. What is your secret life like? What do you like best about it? What do you hate about it? Have you ever let anyone see it? Do you feel at home with it? Are you proud of it? What would like you change in it?

4. Do you nurture the little child you once were and, to a large degree, still are? Do you pay attention to him or her? Do you listen to his or her needs? Do you give yourself time to pretend with, dream with, play with him or her? Do you allow yourself to be touched by his or her innocence?

5. Do you relate to God as a child does to his or her parents? Do you think of God as caring for and providing for all of your needs? Do you ever picture yourself being held by God? If not, what prevents you from doing so?

The Fourth Leg

THE MARK OF CAIN

Be starved in i
as-ha!-sin-ate
my brother-brain
e-n-t-r-a-i-l-e-d—
he wailed the sky
with smoke . . .
. . . turned red,
refused to keep/
u-n-k-e-p-t. un-
Abled-dead, he
stained the sod;
Be marked my head to Nod:
"ca(i)nnot-Be-come-un-clod,"
me fled . . .
"may-not-Be-sod,"
Be bled . . .

—Dennis Billy, "cain"[1]

65

Seldom does our journey pass without difficulty. Petty annoyances get in the way and remind us that our weaknesses are not as easily overcome as we would like. The shadow side of our selves confronts us and, at times, overwhelms us. The sophisticated concerns of daily living interrupt our search for innocence with unexpected, often dangerous detours. We depart from the pilgrim's way and sometimes find it difficult, if not impossible, to get back on track. The failure of such moments threatens and even oppresses us. Whenever its prospect draws near, we run the other way and are willing to do almost anything to avoid having to admit it. When we can no longer elude it, we cut our losses and employ a different tactic. We save face by deflating the significance of our mistake. We blame someone else. We pretend not to care. We deceive ourselves by trying to live a lie.

Most of us care as much about our failures as we do our successes (and perhaps more!). The fear of failure fuels our drive for success. We fear failure so much because we find it hard to believe that we are worth anything apart from our accomplishments: we convince ourselves that we *are* what we do. Since we are so busy doing things, however, we have little time to delve beneath the surface of our actions and discover who we really are and where this or any leg of our journey is taking us.

The Mark of Cain

Cain is the example par excellence of someone who does not deal well with failure (See Gen 4:1–16). He becomes angry and downcast when his offering to Yahweh is not accepted like that of his brother Able. His mood spills over into action and seals his fate. We are never told why one brother's sacrifice is accepted and the other's is not. We are only informed of the tragic results: Cain lures his brother into the open country and kills him. He denies his crime, but is accused by the sound of his brother's blood crying out from the ground, and Yahweh sentences him to a life of senseless wandering in the land of Nod. Cain's murder of his brother expands the spiral of shame that was unleashed by Adam's sin. The failure of Cain reaps a fourfold madness: violence, denial, guilt, and confusion. Such are the consequences of one who surrenders to the savage instincts of human nature: ". . . is not sin at the door like a crouching beast hungering for you?" (Gen 4:7).

There is something of Cain in each of us. Part of us cannot live with failure, and so we blame others for our lack of success. Rather than mastering the beast who lurks beneath the surface of our skin, we let loose its wrath on those around us, often on those closest to us. We envy their prosperity. We are jealous of their accomplishments. We secretly curse them. We may even wish them dead. Enraged by our own lack of good fortune, we become capable of almost anything. Nothing is beneath us. All things are possible, even the most cruel and insensitive of actions. We act out our feelings in various ways and then deny we ever had them. We refuse to accept the consequences of our actions. We fail precisely by our refusal to face our failures and we content ourselves with dragging others down with us. We bear the mark of Cain in our lives: not on our heads, but in our hearts.

A Law Unto Oneself

Rodion Romanovich Raskolnikov, the main character in Dostoyevsky's nineteenth-century Russian novel *Crime and Punishment* (1866), is a typical example of someone who bears the mark of Cain in his heart. A university student with meager means to realize his high ambitions, he convinces himself through a series of daring rational compromises that he has the moral right to kill a miserly old pawnbroker, steal her hoarded fortune, and use it for his own noble purposes. Once in possession of the old woman's money, Raskolnikov plans to finish his university studies in St. Petersburg, establish himself in a career that would be worthy of his talents, and then perform hundreds upon hundreds of good deeds for the benefit of humankind. Killing the old woman, in his mind, is not a crime, but a moral necessity: " For one life, thousands of lives saved from ruin and collapse. One death and a hundred lives—there's arithmetic for you!"[2] He even publishes an article in a prestigious Russian journal, where he expounds the theory that certain extraordinary people (like himself) are endowed with natural rights permitting them to go beyond the strictures of the moral code.

Armed with such rational defenses, Raskolnikov overcomes his initial fears and musters enough nerve to move forward with his plan. He knocks on the pawnbroker's door, invites himself in, brings his ax out from under his coat, and takes her by surprise. As luck would have it, no sooner has he split open the old hag's skull than everything in his plan (indeed in his whole life) falls apart. He cannot find the money right away; Lizaveta, the old woman's simpleminded sister wanders in unexpectedly and suffers a heavy blow from his ax. He then panics and barely escapes the scene of the double murder. In the end, Raskolnikov has killed two people and has hardly anything to show for it. Worse still, he is not at all prepared for the terrible psychological and spiritual effects of his wrongdoing. Within no time, he enters a deep state of depression and takes to bed for weeks, suffering from what appears to be a psychosomatic reaction to his deeds. For the rest of the novel he is lost in an intense state of melancholy.

Raskolnikov must live with the shameful memories of his offense for the rest of his life. He relives those few fatal moments over and over in his mind, again and again, until he can no longer take it: "'I should have known,' he thought with a bitter smile. 'And how did I dare, when I knew myself, when I had the *feeling*, take that ax and shed blood! I should have known beforehand. . . . Ah, but I did know beforehand!' he whispered in despair."[3] Despair is Raskolnikov's punishment for his crime. His unwillingness to confront his failure compounds his guilt and turns him into a suspicious, self-conscious loner. Driven by guilt, a veritable victim of his own crime, he eventually turns himself in and is sentenced to eight years of hard labor in Siberia. Suffering alone will clear his conscience, ease his pain, and offer him the faint hope of redemption.

Self-Deceptions

As Svidrigailov (to Raskolnikov) wisely observes, "Every man thinks of himself; he is happiest who knows best how to pull the wool over his own eyes."[4] So Raskolnikov involves himself in a series of self-deceptions that lead him down the long, hapless road of suspicion and isolation. He convinces himself that he has a right to something that is not his. He plans the murder with care down to the finest details and musters enough nerve to execute his plan. Even though something goes wrong, he still covers up the evidence of his crime with the same meticulous regard for detail. He manages to erase every trace of the crime—every trace, that is, but the evidence that remains burned forever into the deepest recesses of his heart. The memory of his crime is something that he can never hide from or run away from. No matter where he goes, no matter what he does, no matter what he says or does not say, he knows that he has killed. The blood of two women will be forever on his hands. Even the cold of Siberia will not allow him to forget.

Part of the reason why so many of us have a difficult time owning up to our failures and shortcomings is because, like Raskolnikov, we are so good at deceiving ourselves into thinking that there really is nothing to worry about. We see what we want to see and we have a great propensity for rationalizing our behavior in such a way that we justify what we should be ashamed of. Serious flaws of character are viewed as something we can do nothing about, let alone control. Prejudices and biases are justified on moral grounds. Loose and immoral behavior is permitted in the name of individual rights and freedom of expression. Sins against God, against others, against ourselves are seldom, if ever, recognized.

How do we account for such a sad state of affairs? What is it that makes us act this way? How do we explain ourselves? Such questions evoke no easy answers. Perhaps we have lost a sense of sin in our lives. Perhaps our consciences have been numbed by the pervasive presence of our own inhumanity. Perhaps we simply no longer care about doing what is good and right. Whatever the cause, it is obvious we have become masters at pulling the wool over our eyes. Like Raskolnikov and Cain, his scriptural forebear, we have become the undisputed masters of the art of self-deception. If we want, we can deceive ourselves into believing the most preposterous of schemes. We can convince ourselves that we are what we are not. We can rationalize our attitudes and actions away until what once may have been troublesome to us becomes minute and insignificant.

A scene from Dostoyevsky's *The Idiot* (1868-69) comes to mind. The guests at a birthday party decide to take turns, each telling "...whatever he honestly felt in his conscience was the worst of all the bad actions he ever committed in the whole course of his life."[5] Although all is supposed to be done honestly and with no lying, it soon becomes clear that no one is really willing to confess publicly the most hidden and secret embarrassments of his or her life. One confesses a petty theft; another, a failure that actually edifies his character; yet another changes his mind and politely declines to participate. The game, of course, is preposterous, since no one in his or her right mind is going to divulge the truth in such a public forum. That they are even willing to play the game, however, shows how easy it is for them to ignore the truth about themselves and to blur the distinction between reality and illusion. Isn't it the same way with us? Are we who we say we are? Are not most of us involved in a great parlor game of life, where we constantly deceive ourselves into thinking that we are what we are not and where we conveniently overlook the darker, secret side of our natures?

True Confessions

The main difference between Cain and Raskolnikov has to do with 'fessing up to one's failures. Cain wanders the earth with the indelible mark of shame because he refuses to admit his crime and accept the consequences of his actions. Raskolnikov starts out like Cain, but gradually undergoes a change of heart that opens his eyes to the horror of his deeds and what they have made of him. A key element in his conversion is the confession he makes to Sonia, the woman who loves him with all her heart and who follows him through thick and thin. With her help, he is able to pierce through the vast array of self-deceptions that keeps him from the truth about himself and confront the deepest, darkest reality about himself:

> I put up with all this torment of chatter, Sonia, and I wanted to shrug it all off. I wanted to kill without casuistry, to kill for myself, for myself alone! I didn't want to lie about it even to myself! I didn't kill to help my mother—that's rubbish! And I didn't kill to provide myself with means and power for becoming a benefactor to mankind. Rubbish! I simply killed; I killed for myself, for myself alone. Whether I'd become anybody's benefactor or spend my whole life like a spider catching everybody in my web and sucking the living juices out of them—at the moment it should have been all the same to me! ... And, Sonia, when I killed—money wasn't the main thing I needed. It wasn't money I needed, it was something else. ... I had to know, and I had to know right away: was I a louse like all the rest, or was I a man? Could I transgress, or could I not? Did I dare to stoop and

take, or didn't I? Was I mere trembling flesh, or did I
have the right? ... There was just one thing I wanted
to prove to you: that the Devil led me on, and then he
made it clear to me I didn't have the right, because
I'm exactly the same species of louse as all the rest![6]

Once Raskolnikov has admitted his darkest deed to another person, he begins to let go of the guilt and shame
that imprisons him. He is able to stand erect, gradually confront the seriousness of the terrible crime he has committed and accept the consequences. Sonia's words to him
prove prophetic: "You must accept suffering and redeem
yourself by it; that's what you must do."[7] Although he finds
these words hard to accept at first, he eventually embraces
them as the only hope left to him. They are what move him
to embrace the cross of suffering in expiation for his sins
against God and against humanity.

The Shadow of Calvary

Before he turns himself in to the authorities, Raskolnikov
puts Sonia's cross around his neck and remembers some of
her last words to him: "Go to the crossroads, bow down to
the people, kiss the earth because you have sinned against
it, too, and say aloud to the whole world: 'I am a murderer.'"[8]
Raskolnikov is at an important juncture of his life, since his
decision to turn himself in will determine whether the mark
of Cain will be forever cut into his heart or gradually be dis-
placed by the deep purging effects of suffering. In choosing
the latter, Raskolnikov faces his guilt and takes great strides
to overcome it. As the events of his life unfold, one kind of
suffering mysteriously gives way to another.

The glory of Easter does not come without a price. Sooner or later, the shadow of Calvary must cross everyone's path.
For Raskolnikov, it was a long, harrowing journey from the
denial of his crime to the confession of his guilt. For the
women he killed, it was a sudden and violent death at the

hands of a crazed intellectual. For each of us, it will be an intensely personal experience in our lives that will engrave the mark of Christ in our hearts. "If a man wishes to come after me, he must deny his very self ... " (Mk 8:34). "From the cup I drink of you shall drink" (Mk 10:39). "Father, take this cup away from me (Mk 14:36). "I am thirsty" (Jn 19:28). *"Eloi, Eloi, lama sabachthani?"* (Mk 15:34). Only by plumbing the depths of Jesus' suffering and death will we ever grasp the meaning of our own and find the grace to move beyond it. His death promises to heal the deep wounds in our spirits and souls. Planted in the dust of Adam's skull, the tree of Golgotha, "the place of the skull," seeks to penetrate our minds and make its way into the driest and most desolate corners of our hearts. It will not, however, force its way through the hardened soil of doubt and suspicion. We must allow it to break up the ground of our self-identity and penetrate the soil of our most cherished possessions. "He who seeks only himself brings himself to ruin, whereas he who brings himself to nought for me discovers who he is" (Mt 10:39).

Pondering our mortality is certainly not the most comfortable of pastimes. Reflecting on our death, however, brings perspective to our lives and helps us to appreciate more fully the present moment. In a world so heavily focused on the rational, it allows us to get in touch with some of the deepest longings of the human spirit. Even though we encounter death all around us—in the news, in the loss of a family member or friend, on the streets of our cities—there is a part of us that thinks: "Not me! Death happens to other people. I will not die." We deceive ourselves into thinking that an exception will be made for us. We secretly believe we are immortal. We want to be "... like the gods" (Gn 3:5). Because we refuse to deal with death during life, death, at the end of life, will engage with us on its own devastating terms.

Why are we so afraid of death? Because it confronts us with the one limitation we cannot overcome: our own humanity. Death strips from us the masks of our self-deceptions and leaves us naked before ourselves and before our God. It offers us a mirror by which we examine our lives and see the reflection of the self we have become during our journey through time. Many of us are afraid of death because we cannot cope with even the thought of having to face who and what we really are. That's where the cross of Christ comes in. Jesus embraces our suffering in his and lifts it up with his own onto the wood of his cross. His tortured and bloodied body gives meaning to our suffering by immersing us in the harsh, cold realities of life; it cuts through our self-deceptions and enables us to see the naked truth about ourselves: "One day I shall die. What is now *my* flesh and blood, *my* bones and tendons, will turn to dust—and be no more." In the death of Jesus the experience of suffering takes on deeper significance. To live in the shadow of the cross is to carry the mark of Christ in our hearts and to allow its quiet presence to wash clean and wipe out forever the delirious effects of our self-centered lives. It teaches us that we must accept the enigma of suffering in our lives before we can hope to share in the urgency and joy of the empty tomb.

Conclusion

Very little separates us from Cain, our disgraced forebear. The circumstances might be different; the specific intentions and actions might vary; the consequences, however, are the same: violence, denial, guilt, confusion. Have these not been humanity's constant companions throughout its history? Do they not haunt the human family down to the very present? Have the children of Adam fared any better than his firstborn son? The mark of Cain is an emblem of cowardice. His tragic reaction to failure compounded his guilt and turned him into a hapless wanderer of few friends and poor moral stature. His inability to face failure squarely and resolutely cost him dearly for the rest of his life. It takes little knowledge of human nature to understand that what happened to him could also happen to us, that his lonely journey through life could just as easily be ours.

In one way or another, all of us bear the mark of Cain in our lives and must live with the devastating consequences of our selfish actions. Like Raskolnikov, we normally go through a calculated process of denial, escape, and self-deception that does nothing but increase our isolation from others and immerses us in a vast web of poorly reasoned compromises. The illness from which we suffer cannot be cured by pills, or medical treatment, or any other useful prescription for bodily health. It cannot be cured in this way because we suffer not from a physical ailment but from a spiritual malaise that reaches down to the roots of our souls. Like Raskolnikov, we must go through a long and harrowing spiritual and psychological journey to find a cure for the guilt and shame that binds us. Whether or not we find a cure depends greatly on the attitude we take toward our failures and whether or not we are willing to lay down our burdens under the sign of the cross and allow Jesus to burn the mark of discipleship into our hearts. That mark goes deeper than that of Cain and extends to everyone, regardless of who they are and whatever shameful crimes they have yet to confess.

Travel Questions

1. How do you react in times of moral failure? Do you rationalize the situation? Do you find a scapegoat or an excusing clause? Or do you face up to the situation, admit your guilt, and accept the consequences of your actions?

2. In what ways have you given in to the forces of self-deception? What masks do you wear to deceive yourself and others? Have you ever considered yourself a law unto yourself? If not, then whose rule do you live by?

3. Do you ever confess your faults to others? Or do you lock them up inside of you and allow them to torment you in silence and raise their ugly heads in other areas of your life?

4. What does the failure of the cross mean to you? Do you sense any connection between what Jesus went through

and your own journey through life? What does the experience of the cross mean for your daily life?

5. Are you following the way of Cain or the way of the
Lord? The way of self-deception or the way of selfhood?
Can you think of any decisive moments in your life that
determined the direction you have taken?

JOURNEY OF THE HEART

We are the hollow men
We are the stuffed men
Leaning together
Headpiece filled with straw. Alas!
Our dried voices, when
We whisper together
Are quiet and meaningless
As wind in dry grass
Or rats' feet over broken glass
In our dry cellar . . .

—T. S. Eliot, "The Hollow Men"[1]

How do we tear off the masks of self-deception in order to see more clearly the path of the journey before us? How do we break out of the downward spiral of illusionary evil that threatens us at every turn with the loss of what is most precious and dear to us? How do we cope with the nagging fear that we may never even finish what we have started and thus reach the end of our lives with empty hands and nothing to show for all our toil? Prophets and sages have offered a twofold response to this common pilgrim's lament: listen to the still, small voice that rises within your heart; and follow it day by day, one step at a time, until your journey's end. This is easier said than done, of course, and we sometimes fail miserably. Those of us who have tried realize that we need another's help even when following these simple, ordinary steps. We recognize also that for all the intense preparations and practical decision-making involved, the pilgrim's journey is first and foremost a movement within the heart. The reflection offered on this leg of our journey explores the myriad ways of the heart that lead us homeward.

The Voice of the Poet

Emptiness, brokenness, and loneliness have found their way into the deepest recesses of our souls. We do not know how they got there or from whence they came; we know only the pain they bear and the havoc they wreak. Their voices haunt us and leave us little time for sleep. On their account, we do not know who we are or why we are here; we do not know where we are going or what direction we should take. We mirror the drab, colorless surroundings of the lackluster world we inhabit; we crowd together for fleeting comforts and the illusion of security; we feed ourselves with broken promises and lingering self-deceptions. Ours is a sorrowful plight, one that reaches deep into the cellar of our souls, where rats scatter the pieces of our fragmented selves and leave their filthy refuse in the sorrowful ruins of the heart. We move about every which way in a cold and dreary world that is wildly indifferent to our complaints and openly hostile to the deepest longings of our hearts. Afraid of walking a solitary path, we dare not venture beyond the safe, unexamined regulations of the herd. We lean upon each other, always within whisper's reach, forever listening to the cacophony of dull, droning voices that preserves for us the illusion of living.

The opening passage of Eliot's "The Hollow Men" articulates this unspoken, often unconscious, aching of the human heart as it seeks to find its way through the cold, meandering maze of inner disquiet. The heart has not fared well along the way. Stuck in a quagmire of rational confusions and compromising doubts, it has become uncertain of its own powers to orient aright and steer to safe haven those who dare to long for something more in life. Such persistent self-examination has even brought into question its own existence. "The heart," a friend of mine from college once told me, "is a hollow muscular organ that pumps blood through our arteries and veins—nothing more, nothing less!" End of the discussion. How do you discuss "matters of heart" with someone who wants to examine everything under a microscope and break down what he or she finds there into its most basic chemical compounds?

The Analogy of Heart

My friend would much rather have dissected a bodily organ than to have listened to my questions about human existence. He reduced all of life to mere flesh and bones—and was adamant about it! Although there was no arguing with him, I do not see how his narrow, physicalist outlook on life could have satisfied his deepest, innermost longings and, to be honest, I am not thoroughly convinced that he actually believed it himself. I suspect he was deceiving himself and others by running away from the affective side of his personality, something all to easy to do in a world that places such a high value on lofty cerebral calculations. When it suits us, most of us have a similar talent for trivializing our fears and then rationalizing them away to the point of absurdity. Why deal with matters of the heart when doing so will force us to question some of our most basic assumptions about who we are and how we live our lives? Calling "a spade a spade" or, by way of analogy, "a heart a heart" makes things much simpler for all concerned—or, at least, so some people, like my friend, seem somehow to have convinced themselves.

Life, however, is rarely so neat and tidy. Time and time again, it evades our best efforts to harness its wild and unruly forces. Just when we think we have seized the day and taken the bull by the horns, something unexpected happens that causes the entire situation to change: the ground mysteriously shifts; someone or something pushes us off balance; we lose our footing, slip, and fall; the bull suddenly gets a second wind. Anything can happen! Better to be prepared for the unexpected than caught off guard at the most inopportune moment.

The harsh daily realities of life in the modern world require us to take a second look at facile rationalizations about the spiritual dimensions of the human heart. A physicalist approach may suffice for the research lab or operating table, but it cannot even begin to cope with the all the nitty-gritty, messy details of life on this sorrowful and lackluster planet of ours. To do so, we need to understand that words carry with them not one, but a variety of related meanings.

So it is with our common, everyday word *heart*. We use it in so very many ways. Someone has "captured our heart" or "broken our heart." We speak of "heart and soul," "heart and mind," and "heart and strength." We "give our hearts away," and we describe someone as "not having a heart." When using phrases such as these, most of us don't need to be told that we are referring to something more than the physical heart itself, that we, in fact, mean much more by these phrases than what the physicalist attitude suggests. We know that we are using a metaphor to give concrete shape to an emotional experience and that we are drawing a very basic comparison between our bodily existence and our inner, psychic life: the physical heart assures the flow of blood and thereby represents the seat of life; "heart" as found in the above phrases describes the steady flow of our emotions and represents the seat of our affective life.

A man or woman of "heart" is a compassionate person, someone able to sympathize with others in a way that brings about a deep and authentic sharing of self. He or she is capable of listening to the concerns of others and possesses the rare talent of being able to forget himself or herself in the midst of life's difficulties. There are different degrees of "heart," ranging anywhere from calculated altruism to reciprocated trust to selfless compassion. During our lifetimes most of us wander somewhere in the middle ground, hoping to hit the mark, but all too often falling miserably short of it. As with most other things in life, the key question here is whether we are making any headway. When it comes to matters of the heart, the measure of growth is far more important than any isolated instance of success or failure.

A Crisis of Heart

These rather benign descriptions of "heart" do not, of course, belie the deep spiritual crisis that has recently taken hold of our souls. The fragmentation of culture in Western society over the last one hundred years has taken its toll on the inner reserves of the heart. Never before have people experienced themselves in such a broken and fragmented state. The distance between mind and heart has become so vast that the effort to integrate the two has become an arduous, lifelong task. So deep have the emotions been repressed that many people do not know how to listen to their feelings anymore, let alone accept what they are trying to tell them about their lives and then change their lives accordingly.

The crisis is not merely a matter of putting the fragmented pieces of self back together, as if one were fitting together the pieces of a puzzle or assembling a model boat or airplane. Would that it were so easy! Nor is it merely a matter of missing a few pieces of the puzzle, either through neglect or through temporary misplacement. Even this difficulty could be resolved once the puzzle takes on shape and its design becomes more easily recognizable. In such cases, those putting the puzzle together have an idea of the whole before they start. They know what it is *supposed* to look like and set out to construct it accordingly, missing pieces or no missing pieces! The present crisis has more to do with having lost the sense of the whole toward which we are working.

With no little or no idea of just where our emotions fit into our lives, we have lost touch with them and perceive them as unrelated, isolated passions that rebel against reason, demand instant gratification, and are controlled only with great, superhuman acts of will. An endless chain of fragmented uncertainties convinces us that there is nothing we can do about this hopeless situation. As a result, we either repress our emotions so completely that we are no longer conscious of them, or we fall entirely under their sway, with no possibility of exerting any manageable control over them.

Two prime examples of society's crisis of heart appear in Weston and Devine, the antagonists in C.S. Lewis' science fiction novella, *Out of the Silent Planet*. Forged together by their common purpose to exploit the resources of the distant planet Malacandra (i.e., Mars), these unlikely partners—one a thoroughgoing empiricist, the other an out-and-out epicurean—stop short of nothing to fulfill their plans of unrivaled wealth and glory. Completely cut off from their own inner worlds, they travel to this pristine, unfallen planet, equipped with the latest scientific theories and the best technology of their day. As the plot thickens, however, it soon becomes clear that they have also brought with them a plethora of distorted values and inverted priorities that, if left unchecked, will surely land Malacandra in a murky swamp of premeditated and participated evils. Toward the end of the novel, Weston expounds his warped philosophy of life:

> Life . . . has ruthlessly broken down all obstacles and liquidated all failures and today in her highest form— civilized man—and in me as his representative, she presses forward to that interplanetary leap which will, perhaps, place her for ever beyond the reach of death. . . . It is her right, . . . the right, or, if you will, the might of Life herself, that I am prepared without flinching to plant the flag of man on the soil of Malacandra: to march on, step by step, superseding, where necessary, the lower forms of life that we find, claiming planet after planet, system after system, till our posterity—whatever strange form and yet unguessed mentality they have assumed—dwell in the universe wherever the universe is habitable.[2]

Weston is the example par excellence of the physicalist approach to life. Dedicating his life to the preservation of his race and a notion of progress that has gone strangely awry, he will use whatever means necessary to achieve his ends, regardless of its effect on others. Devine, his entrepreneuring accomplice, is, on the other hand, propelled by the pursuit of wealth and the pleasure it can buy. He admits his own spiritual bankruptcy—and Weston's—but simply does not care. Both Weston and Devine have repressed their emotions to such an extent that they are unable to recognize their own human impoverishment. Since neither acknowledges the relevance of heart, their presence in whatever world they inhabit will always be a strong obstacle to those on the side of good. They have explored the farthest reaches of space, but have not the slightest clue how to embark on that interior journey that will lead them to a deep sense of their own human frailty. They have turned their fleshy hearts to stone and now seek to impose their weight and influence on others. To us, they are a blunt reminder of our own potential for evil and a negative example of what we ourselves can all too easily become.

The Open Heart

We should be grateful that Weston and Devine are not the only alternatives open to us. In a time of crisis as deep and as threatening as our own, good and evil confront each other on open ground and forge from their intense struggle an array of new possibilities. Where matters of heart are concerned, any tragedy or crisis presents a person with the opportunity to explore previously uncharted corners of his or her heart and to experience, as if for the first time, feelings and emotions that otherwise would have been casually overlooked or disposed of. A tragedy in a person's life can sensitize a person to the reality of suffering not only in his or her life, but in the lives of those around them, and often even in the lives of people they have never even seen.

Take, for example, the tragic story of Etty Hillesum, a Dutch Jew who died at Auschwitz on November 30, 1943, and who has left through her diaries an endearing testimony of the spiritual journey of the soul in the face of the greatest adversities. Published in English in 1983 as *An Interrupted Life: The Diaries of Etty Hillesum 1941–43,* the eight exercise books of this young aspiring writer reveal a sensitivity to the inner landscape of her soul. She writes about what most other people simply ignore, sensing that " . . . it is possible to create, even without ever creating a word or painting a picture, by simply moulding one's inner life."[3] She sees the importance of nurturing the heart with prayer, realizing that "... sometimes the most important thing in a whole day is the rest we take between two deep breathes, or the turning inwards in prayer for five short minutes."[4] Her inward journey gave her a deep awareness and appreciation of the world around her. Even the imminent threat of Nazi occupation and deportation does not make her lose her orientation and sense of place in life:

> I took the blackout paper down from the window and suddenly there were two stars at the head of the bed. They were not the same stars I see through my window but I felt in touch with them all the same, and suddenly I was quite certain that no matter where I was in the world I would always find stars and be able to flop down on a bed, or on a floor, or anywhere else, and feel absolutely at home.[5]

Looking at the stars, Etty sees a reflection of her own inner life and realizes that, no matter what happens, no one can snatch her away from the arms of God. This powerful intuition enables her to open her heart to the stars, to the world about her, to her family and friends who share her plight, to her suffering people, even to the German soldiers who are persecuting them: "There are no frontiers between suffering people, and we must pray for them all."[6] She learns the importance of clearing "... a decent shelter for your sorrow ..." rather than reserving "... most of the space inside you for hatred and thoughts of revenge...."[7] Most importantly, she senses the strong connection between prayer and coping with the adversities of life: "I draw prayer round me like a dark protective wall, withdraw inside it as one might into a convent cell and then step outside again, calmer and stronger and more collected again."[8] In the midst of adversity, Etty Hillesum turned inward and was still able to find wonder and beauty in life. She did not complain about her sufferings, but sensed that somehow, in spite of it all, perhaps even *because* of it all, God was especially close, so close that he could almost be touched. What Etty struggled so desperately to put into

words and to live out in her life in the smallest details gives
eloquent testimony to the great strength and resiliency of
the human heart. It also reveals what anyone who takes the
time to listen to his or her heart already knows for sure:
"The Lord is close to the broken heart" (Ps 34:18).

The Heart of Jesus

What does it mean to say that God is close to the broken heart? Does it simply mean that we are on God's mind,
that in some strange way God pays more attention to those
whose hearts have been stretched to the point of breaking? Does it mean that God pays us some kind of a special
visit, as if we were sick in the hospital and in need of someone to hold our hands or to give us words of comfort?
Does it mean that God simply encourages us to be patient
until things will get better or strengthens us by his grace to
endure whatever suffering still lies ahead? Yes and no. Yes,
because each of these descriptions says something at least
partially true about the way God relates to us. No, because
God does so very much more. The figure of Jesus' bloodied corpus hanging from the cross draws back the hidden
veil of divinity and reveals that God has come to us and
drawn near to us in order to suffer *with* us. Through his
suffering and death, Jesus unites our fragmented and broken hearts to his own and gives all who suffer there a deeper understanding of his divine compassion.

"My God, my God, why have you forsaken me?" Jesus
cried (Mk 15:34). We make a mockery of God's love for us
if we portray it in a way that minimizes the great amount
of physical, psychological, and spiritual anguish that Jesus
went through during his earthly passion. Betrayed by one
of his closest followers, deserted by the others, spat upon
and mocked, stripped of his clothes, beaten and scourged,
nailed to a cross to suffer a criminal's death, Jesus ended
his life on earth a defeated and broken man. The sense of
disgrace and public embarrassment, the intense isolation

and feeling of failure, the loss of hope and experience of abandonment weighed heavily on his heart and must have heightened his physical torments beyond all imagination. Time itself slowed for him as seconds seemed like hours and as the hours themselves stretched to the point of breaking. In those few hours on the cross, Jesus embraced the sufferings of the whole world. He emptied himself so that he could be filled with the world's brokenness and, in doing so, made himself present for ages to come wherever and whenever a tear of anguish was shed or an aching heart broken for lack of love.

"Though he was able to save us in a thousand ways, he chose the most humiliating and painful way of dying on the cross of pure suffering,"[9] wrote St. Alphonsus Liguori, giving us a sense of the absurd steps that God has taken to manifest his love for us. The bloodied corpus of Jesus hanging from the grimy wood of a Roman crossbeam between two criminals shows us that God loves us not from afar, not in the abstract spheres of speculative thought, not as a kindly visitor from across the threshold of time, but to the point of dying for us. By becoming flesh and embracing our suffering on the ignominy of the cross, God has drawn near to us and has forever united us to himself: our own suffering is now his suffering; his compassion, now our own; his heart, our heart; his touch, our touch. The words of Thomas Merton come to mind:

> If my compassion is true, if it be a deep compassion of the heart and not a legal affair, or a mercy learned from a book and practiced on others like a pious exercise, then my compassion for others is God's mercy for me. My patience with them is His patience with me. My love for them is His love for me.[10]

"Christ," he goes on to say, "cannot love without feeling and without heart."[11] Nor can we. The paradox of the cross is that Christ's suffering and his compassion are now mysteriously manifested in our own. The heart of Jesus now extends itself to every human heart, and in every human heart there can be found an echo, however faint, of the dying, suffering of Christ.

Conclusion

During his lifetime Jesus is said to have exorcised demons, healed people of the physical and spiritual maladies, and even awakened people from the sleep of death. The power of his words was such that they effected precisely what he signified by them—to the great astonishment of his hearers. Can the power of Jesus' words reach across the centuries and perform in this desolate world of ours what it accomplished in the syncretic religious atmosphere of first century Palestine? Can the hollow men, the stuffed men of Eliot's poem be awakened from their droning slumber? Can the cellars of their souls be swept clean of the broken glass? Can their whispers turn to song, their headpieces of straw become integrated minds and hearts? Answers to such questions ultimately turn on faith.

Today we have no other recourse than to journey inward and to seek to listen to the still, small voice of God in our hearts. Only there, in the stillness and lonely solitude of our hearts, will we find a place where we are embraced and invited, ever so slowly, to turn our hearts outward and to share that embrace with others. If figures like Weston and Devine remind us of the difficulty—even impossibility—of such a task, the gentle and moving testimony of an Etty Hillesum shows us that, even in the darkest hours of life, the human heart can thrive and extend itself beyond our wildest expectations. Her eloquent story of life's inner journey reminds us of the task each of us has: to look within our hearts and to find there, in the midst of our broken and fragmented hearts, a place of healing, a place of rest.

Jesus' brokenness on the cross invites us to get in touch with our own broken humanity and to deliver it up to his selfless embrace. His heart is big enough to hold and to heal any open, festering wound that life can deal out to us. It is also small enough to make us feel at home with our humanity and not overawed by the depths of his affection. The Word of God crossed the threshold of eternity and gave us Jesus so that we would never again have to doubt the depths of God's love for us. Through Jesus of Nazareth that same Word of God reaches through the portal of time itself and offers us down through the centuries a place of healing and badly needed rest. Today, as always, he offers his embrace to anyone who seeks him with an open, aching heart.

Travel Questions

1. Do you find it easier relating to others with your head or with your heart? Can you name any recent instances when you opened your heart to another? Was it easy or difficult? What prevents you from doing so more often?

2. Do you feel at home with your emotions? Do you usually understand why you feel a certain way? Which emotions do you find the easiest to share? Which do you find the most difficult? Why?

3. What do you do to nurture your heart? Do you do it often? Every now and then? Hardly ever? When was the last time you looked into your heart and thought about your feelings about yourself? About the people you live with? About God?

4. Do you have a sturdy shelter for your joys and sorrows? Do you have an intimate friend with whom you can share the successes and trials of your life? Do you feel free enough to share them with God?

5. Is compassion an important value in your life? Do you normally find it in others? In yourself? In God?

The Sixth Leg

ECHOING THE FAITH

A Sufi Bayazid once said this about himself:

"I was a revolutionary when I was young and all my prayer to God was 'Lord, give me the energy to change the world.'

"As I approached middle age and realized that half my life was gone without my changing a single soul, I changed my prayer to 'Lord, give me the grace to change all those who come in contact with me. Just my family and friends, and I shall be satisfied.'

"Now that I am an old man and my days are numbered, my one prayer is, 'Lord, give me the grace to change myself.' If I had prayed for this right from the start I should not have wasted my life."

—Anthony De Mello,
"Change the World by Changing Me"[1]

Openness of heart leads to conversion of life; the pilgrim's way, to new expressions of holiness. Most of us have probably had one or more experiences in our lives that we look to as a moment of grace, as a time of conversion. Some of us may even measure our lives by moments such as these. These are very private, personal experiences. They are difficult to share, but share them we must. For they really belong to all of us. They are *our* stories, the stories of the church, the stories of our Lord's dealings with us at our present moment in history. All we can really do is say what happened: give our testimony, tell our stories of how the Lord has come to us.

The gospels and the Acts of the Apostles are full of such accounts of personal conversion: Peter (Jn 18:12-27; 21:15-23), Paul (Acts 9:1-19), Mary Magdalen (Lk 8:1-3), Zacchaeus (Lk 19:1-10), to name just a few. Jesus himself left us such powerful parables of conversion as "The Lost Sheep" (Mt 18:12-14), "The Pharisee and the Publican" (Lk 18:9-14), and "The Prodigal Son" (Lk 15:11-32).

When you get right down to it, all of these tales make the same basic point: to be converted means that God has moved from the periphery to the center of one's life. This shift means letting go, willingly placing ourselves on the edge, allowing God's ways to become our ways. Easier said than done. Conversion is no piece of cake. We know we cannot do it alone. We cannot, in fact, do it at all. We must rely completely on God's help, and our intuition tells us that very often God chooses to help us through the words and actions of others.

A Moment of Conversion

On this leg of our journey, I would like to share with you an experience from my life that has had a lasting impression on me, one I will never forget. It is the story of my conversion.

I feel a little embarrassed having to admit that once, a long time ago, I almost left the Catholic Church. In the fall of 1971, I entered my freshman year at Dartmouth College in New Hampshire. Tucked away in the northern woods of New England—away from "the real world" as so many of us used to put it—Dartmouth students had earned a reputation of being men (I was a member of the last all-male class to matriculate there) who studied hard, loved their sports, and partied to their hearts' content. We took pride in our unofficial nickname, "The Dartmouth Animals."

Now, I would like you to believe that I went there only to study and to perfect the art of long-distance running on The Big Green Machine's cross-country team ("The Big Green" was another one of our fanciful, but this time official, college nicknames). But I have to admit that, along with most of my other freshmen classmates, I went to my fair share of fraternity rushes and Saturday night bashes. I remember waking up on one or two Sunday mornings with a terrible splitting headache. No need to go into any of the grimy details; let it simply be said that during my first year of college I was in grave danger of becoming what Thomas Merton liked to call "a frat rat."

That first year was exciting, but also very troubling for me. It was the first time in my life that I was away from my family and friends for any extended period. Coming out of a Catholic elementary and high school system, where I was educated by the Presentation Sisters of the Blessed Virgin Mary and the Irish Christian Brothers, respectively, it was also the first time in my life that I found some of my most basic assumptions about life, about religion, and about God challenged, not so much by my professors (although one or two of them managed to get under my skin), but by my classmates. Being in an environment where not everyone was Catholic, where not everyone was Christian, where not everyone believed in God, and where some people did not seem to believe in anything at all, was very confusing to me. Easily influenced by my peers, I felt a little over-whelmed by it all.

At first, I played the role of an apologist and tried to defend what I had always been told to believe. That did not last very long. The arguments of my classmates were too good for me. I could not keep up with them and, after a while, they even started to make sense. I had no answers that would satisfy them, and, gradually, my answers did not even satisfy mc. Then some of my Catholic classmates, from whom I expected more support, began to change. Some started smoking marijuana. Others experimented with some of the Eastern religions; others, with Christian fundamentalism. Others stopped believing in God alto-gether. And, to be honest, I felt myself drifting in the general same direction—away from the Catholic Church.

And I probably would have were it not for Father Bill Nolan, who at the time was the chaplain at Aquinas House, the Catholic Center at Dartmouth. During the second trimester of my freshman year I found myself wandering into Father Bill's office about once every week or so, main-ly to lock horns with him (I can be pretty engaging when I want to). I gave him all my newfound arguments against God and religion, together with all the things that I could think of that were wrong with the Catholic Church (my list, by this time, had become pretty long), and I tried to convince him that my decision to leave the Catholic Church was mature and well thought-out, that I was fol-lowing my conscience and doing the right thing. In fact, I was looking for a fight. I figured that if I argued with him long enough he would eventually do either one of two things: give up or explode. Either way, I would have won. And, if he exploded, well, that would have been just one more reason for me to leave the church.

The trouble was that I could not get Father Bill to argue back. He explained the church's teaching as best he could. But, other than that, all he did was to keep on saying week after week, time and time again, in his deep voice that exuded confidence, "Now, Dennis, be sure you know what you're rejecting before you toss it all away." After our second or third meeting, I was beginning to get a little annoyed with his unwillingness to engage my arguments head on. I could not draw him into the fray of battle. He just sat there and smiled at me. How do you fight with someone who refuses to fight back? Turning one's cheek in what was supposed to be a serious argument was going a bit too far. The "Golden Rule," I thought, did not apply in matters of such consequence. To tell you the truth, Father Bill took me by surprise with his calm and gentle manner. And, deep down inside, I knew he was right. I could not reject my Catholic faith because even after my Catholic upbringing and education, I really did *not* know what it was all about (and I certainly did not understand it). For all my life, I had simply taken it for granted. And since I could no longer do that, I decided to do something about it.

Over the space of the next six weeks, I read the documents of the Second Vatican Council slowly and with great interest from cover to cover. I still have the copy of the Abbot edition that I read, and I go back to it often to examine all the notes I made in the margins and all the things I underlined because they impressed me so much. I remember, for example, being particularly taken up by the idea of Christ's Body being a complex reality with different degrees of incorporation.[2] I was also very much impressed with the image of the church as "the People of God," with the expressed willingness of the church to enter into dialogue with other Christian and non-Christian faiths, and with its repeated emphasis on the dignity of the human person.[3]

It is difficult to explain, but after reading the documents of the Second Vatican Council, I felt as if I was experiencing my faith for the first time. The pieces were beginning to fit together. It all started to make sense to me. I was beginning to feel something I had not felt in a long time, if ever: at home in my faith. I was no longer taking it for granted. I was beginning to take responsibility for what I believed. And, most importantly, I was beginning to experience God as a personal presence in my life. That is not to say that all my difficulties with the Catholic faith simply melted away. My arguments and objections were not all answered, not by a long shot. But I can honestly say that from pieces strewn throughout the various documents of the Council, I was able to come up with a vision of the Catholic faith that I could readily accept. At the end of that six-week period during my freshman year in college, I consciously chose to remain a member of the Catholic faith—and I have never regretted my decision, not for a single moment.

I look upon my freshman year in college as a quiet time of conversion. During that year I was thinking deep thoughts—as deep as I could go at the time—and renewing my Catholic faith in profound ways. Towards the end of the year, I had an official group interview with Father Bill. (Throughout the year, he had been slowly making his way through the freshman class in small gatherings of five or six.) Toward the end of this meeting, we were each handed an index card and told to write down our name, our college address, our major, if we had one yet, and what we wanted to be. I surprised myself and probably Father Bill as well (although, perhaps not!) when I put down that I wanted to be a priest. I was ordained eight years later.

Personal Conversion

That is the story of my conversion, or at least a part of it. There is nothing very dramatic about it. I share it with you not to make an impression, not even to make a point, but simply because it is my story. I need to tell it. And you, believe it or not, need to hear it. We need to get beneath the appearance of things, to talk about what really matters to us. It is what God wants us to do. It is also what we really want to do, but it is so very, very hard. The priest in George Bernanos' novel *The Diary of a Country Priest* says it best:

> I believe, in fact I am certain, that many of us never give out the whole of ourselves, our deepest truth. We live on the surface, and yet, so rich is the soil of humanity that even this thin outer layer is able to yield a kind of meagre harvest which gives the illusion of real living.[4]

Conversion bids us to go beneath the surface, to let the truths of the faith to become a part of our story, so much so that we will echo our faith for others.

Interestingly enough, when the recently published *Catechism of the Catholic Church* speaks about the process of conversion, it does not try to tantalize us with technical language or innovative theories; it does not leave it on the level of the abstract, as something outside of us and largely unknown to us. No, it refers to a simple story of conversion, a story from the mouth of Jesus himself, a story that is really your story, and my story, the story of the prodigal son. Paragraph 1439 reads thus:

> The process of conversion and repentance was described by Jesus in the parable of the prodigal son, the center of which is the merciful father: the fascination of illusory freedom, the abandonment of the father's house; the extreme misery in which the son finds himself after squandering his fortune; his deep humiliation at finding himself obliged to feed swine, and still worse, at wanting to feed on the husks the pigs ate; his reflection on all he has lost; his repentance and decision to declare himself guilty before his father; the journey back; the father's generous welcome; the father's joy—all these are characteristic of the process of conversion. The beautiful robe, the ring, and the festive banquet are symbols of that new life—pure, worthy, and joyful—of anyone who returns to God

and to the bosom of his family, which is the Church.
Only the heart of Christ who knows the depths of his
Father's love could reveal to us the abyss of his mer-
cy in so simple and beautiful a way.[5]

Jesus' parables go below the surface of life and bid us to
open up and share our own stories of the merciful love of
the Father. They emphasize the importance of changing our
own lives before we even dare think about effecting a conversion in the lives of those around us. "Reform your lives
and believe in the Gospel," the gospel of Mark advises (Mk
1:15). Personal conversion comes prior to societal change—
not vice versa. Therein lies the heart of the matter.

In his book *The God of Surprises,* Gerard W. Hughes
tells how he used to look out from the window of his tower room at a Jesuit retreat house in North Wales and con-
verse with the sprawling valley below him, usually when
he was in a bad mood and wanted to get something off his
chest. Valleys cannot answer back, and this was a way he
could tell the world off, regain a relative sense of quiet in
his life, and go on with his work. But one day, amidst all his
projects for change and other matters of consequence, he
felt as if the valley was talking back to him. He came to a
stark realization:

I began to see that the real battle is not in working to
change the structure of the Church and of society, but
in struggling to change the structure of my psyche.
This may sound very individualistic and selfish, but
the only thing we can change is ourselves, for the only
power that can bring creative change is God. I cannot
domesticate God, I cannot tell him what to do, no
matter how noble the cause: all I can do is let his glory through in me, let God be God in my own life.[6]

We cannot change the world and its structures and the
people in it, if we do not first seek to change ourselves. And
we cannot change ourselves if we do not allow God to do it

for us. "Convert us, Lord, and we will be converted" (Lam 5:21). Like Hughes' tower experience, moments of conversion can come to us at any time—even when we least expect them.

Conclusion

A while back, I had the opportunity to go back to Dartmouth and visit Father Bill. He is retired now, in his late seventies, and has the beginning stages of Alzheimer's. It was a bit emotional for me to see him that way, not only because his health was beginning to fail, but also because we both had always hoped that I would carry on his work at Dartmouth once he retired. Much to my regret, and to his, this was not to be. I was happy that he was able to remember me. He still had that deep voice and gentlemanly manner about him, but it was obvious after only a few minutes that he was beginning to forget things. Forget as he may, I will never forget him, or his gentle manner, or the sound advice he gave me.

When I look at the documents of the Second Vatican Council, I often picture them on his desk as I went to him for my weekly visits. The covers are worn; the pages tattered. I see him opening the Abbot edition and other related works late at night alone in his study, referring to them, pondering them, wondering how he should answer me and all the other students who were questioning their faith. I see him opening these books, not to use them as weapons, but to learn from them so that the truths of the faith would penetrate deep into his heart and echo back for others to hear—as I heard and, I'm sure, so many others heard—the voice of God.

I am now at the beginning of my middle age and, if I am to be honest, I would have to admit that, while I am no longer a revolutionary (if I ever was), much of my life is still caught up in trying to turn the people and structures around me into a glorified image of myself. Sometimes I deceive myself into thinking that I am accomplishing something. At other times, I am able to see with a clearer vision. Most of time, I feel like

I am wandering in a dark room looking for the light switch, which I know is there but cannot seem to find.

Only recently have I come to begin each day with a simple prayer: "Lord, help me to let you be God in my life. Change what you want in me and help me to accept it as your will." Unlike the Sufi Bayazid, whose words grace the opening lines of this short reflection on the meaning of conversion, old age, for me, is still a long way off. Whether I heed his words and avoid wasting the rest of my precious journey through life remains to be seen.

Travel Questions

1. If someone asked you to tell the story of your conversion, which incident or series of incidents from your life would you highlight? Have you ever shared your conversion story with another? If not, why not?

2. Who are the people in your life who have helped you to deepen your faith? How did they help you? Were they aware of it at the time? What was it that touched you most in their ongoing contact with you?

3. Have you yourself ever played an instrumental role in another's conversion? What was it like? How did you feel before, during, and afterwards? Can you think of specific words or actions that you did that made a deep impression on another's belief system?

4. Does conversion come through changing social structures or through changing one's heart? Can you cite specific examples of what you mean? Have you ever had an experience where social structures have gotten in the way of a person's conversion? Have you ever had an experience where they have fostered an atmosphere of interior conversion?

5. Has your understanding of the meaning of conversion changed over the course of the years? If so, in what way has it changed? If not, what are the features that have remained constant throughout?

FRIENDS FOR THE JOURNEY

This I have read in some old book and wise,
Penned long ago by one who understood
The heart of man, and looked with seeing eyes
Upon the world, and evil things and good:
"Here where all changes and naught can endure,"
He wrote, "here where all beauty dwells with pain,
And love which at the first was deep and pure
By love of self is often rendered vain—
Here, when the many meet, they meet to turn
Back from the steep and toilsome upward way;
Few meet to rise together—few, to spurn
That which is base, to work, and climb, and pray.
Precious is friendship when friend calls to friend,
'Be strong! Here is my hand. Let us ascend!'"
—Mary Dixon Thayer, "To Elizabeth"[1]

The longer we journey together, the more we appreciate the companionship of our fellow travelers. Their effect on our lives, while not easily measured, should not go unnoticed. On this leg of our journey, we ponder the gift of those who walk beside us in faith. Without their help, many of us would never find our way home.

A True Story

Not long ago I read a book called *The Long Walk*, a true story of survival which took place in the early years of the Second World War, a story about the escape of seven inmates from a Soviet labor camp in northern Siberia. With only a very few provisions, a blunted ax head, a makeshift knife for protection, and no map or compass to guide them, these poorly-clad prisoners battled the elements and gambled against all the odds in order to have a second lease on life. For fourteen long, burdensome months, they journeyed southward through the desolate tundra of northern Siberia, into Outer Mongolia and the blazing heat of great Gobi desert, through isolated mountain regions of Tibet, across the icy slopes of the Himalayas, and finally to the relatively safe haven of the Indian sub-continent. By all accounts, it was only their strong determination to survive that kept them alive and which also forged among them the bonds of human friendship.

I found the final words of the book particularly touching. Slavomir, the twenty-six year old Polish lieutenant who narrates the story, describes his feelings when he finally has to say goodbye to his closest companion. After all their trials together, after the scorching days and the freezing nights, after all the hunger and thirst, the lack of sleep and the tattered clothing, after all the heartache and the pain, and their many close brushes with death, he found that he was bound to his comrade in a way he could not describe: "The bus pulled away towards the transit camp where I was to await a troopship for the Middle East. I looked back at him once and he waved. I felt suddenly bereft of friends, bereft of everything, as desolate and as lonely as a man could be."[2]

The Walk of Friendship

From the moment of our birth, each of us begins a long walk through life. Call it a journey, a pilgrimage, an adventure, an escape. Whatever you call it, it is just as challenging, just as stretching, just as life-threatening, and just as hopeful as if we ourselves were slushing through the icy Siberian tundra ourselves and making our way southward some three thousand miles. We are on a long walk to freedom. It is our faith in God which gives direction to our journey, which makes sense of it all, which holds us together, which draws us close.

The people we travel with, our friends and companions, give us the concrete support we need to carry on. Some of us may think it possible to go it alone. We may even want to try. But the wisdom of the centuries, the experience of those who have gone before us, and our own inner instincts tell us that we cannot make it on our own.

I wonder if we have ever reflected on the importance of friendship for our lives. The people we live our lives with, the people we love, whom we care for, play with, argue with, fight with, make up with, and carry on with. Do we believe they have become our friends by pure chance? Would anyone else have been just as good? Do we see God's hand at all in the relationships we have formed, in those we choose to recognize as friends?

Perhaps we may feel that we have no real friends. This is becoming more and more of a common feeling in the hustle and bustle of our busy world. One noted sociologist says that members of today's middle class have no close friends. We stop short of committing ourselves fully. We run into an inner barrier and stop. What we have instead are allies or alliances, friendships of utility which we need to survive in today's dangerous world. But that is as far as we are willing to go. We deceive ourselves by mistaking alliances for real friendships, when in truth, they don't even come close.[3]

Perhaps we feel like the character in John Barth's novel *The Floating Opera:* "Our friends float past; we become involved with them; they float on, and we must rely on hearsay or lose track of them completely; they float back again, and we must either renew our friendship—catch up to date—or find that they and we don't comprehend each other any more."[4]

And then there are the prophets of doom. Eli Ginzsburg once likened friendship to a canoe shooting the rapids of the river of change. In his mind, western society is changing so rapidly that pretty soon "we are all going to be anonymous city-dwellers, people without ties or commitments to long-time friends and neighbors."[5] Perhaps we *have* entered the age of "loose ties" and "networking." Perhaps people have developed the ability to form only "buddy-type" relationships on the basis of common interests and loose affiliations, friendships that they will be able to withdraw from all too easily by either moving to another city or by joining a similar interest group in the same location.[6]

If we have difficulty making firm, solid, intimate, lasting friendships, the chances are that our friendship with God has also been left unattended. In the words of Thomas Clancy, "Speaking on intimate terms with God 'exactly as one friend speaks to another,' has yet to be really explored, partly because our personal relationships themselves have become so bland that we have forgotten how intimate friends do speak to one another."[7] Could it be that the saints themselves were able to talk to God in such intimate terms precisely because they themselves were nourished by strong intimate friendships? The lives of saints such as St. Francis of Assisi and St. Clare, St. Francis de Sales and St. Jane de

Chantal, St. Vincent de Paul and St. Louise de Marillac, seem to indicate that this is so.

Perhaps the call to sanctity and the call to friendship are intimately tied to one another. Perhaps to find the one we need to discover, or rediscover, what the other is all about. Perhaps we need to retrieve the wisdom of the past concerning friendship. What does friendship mean? What is distinctive about it? How does it compare with the other forms of love we experience in our lives?

The Threefold Order

To begin with, friendship is a natural love. It differs from simple affection, which stems from natural instincts at work in well-established relationships (such as sibling loyalties; maternal or paternal care, etc.). It also differs from romantic love, which involves sexual attraction and focuses on the mutual experience of "being in love." Friendship, or *philia* as the Greeks called it, is "a close bond between two individuals by virtue of some common interest."[8] It is the most spiritual of the human loves, and can stem from virtually any common interest: stamp-collecting, gardening, or roller coasters!

According to C.S. Lewis, these three natural loves—affection, eros, and friendship—can be transformed by God's grace and turned into modes of charity (*agape*), that sacrificial love which enables us to reach out to everyone, even to those who seem unlovable, while also remaining the natural loves they were.[9] One person who has had a lot to say about the meaning of friendship is the Greek philosopher Aristotle (384-322 B.C.). In his *Nicomachean Ethics*, he describes three different kinds of friendship, each of which stem from one of three motivations: utility, pleasure, and character.[10] Propelled by some vested interest that dictates the parameters of the relationship, we enter into friendships of *utility* in order to get something for ourselves. We become friends with another person only because he or she is of some use to us. When this motivation ceases, so does the friendship.

Friendships of *pleasure*, by way of contrast, develop because we enjoy being in a certain person's company. We like being with a particular individual because he or she makes us laugh, engages us in thoughtful conversation, is good dinner company, etc. We relish being with him or her, and vice versa. Pleasure is the motivation: nothing more; nothing less. In such friendships, we appreciate not the friend, but the pleasure he or she bestows on us.

Despite their familiar presence in our lives, friendships of utility and pleasure fall far short of perfection. When someone no longer benefits us or ceases to evoke any pleasure in us, it is relatively easy for us to stop caring for him or her. These kinds of friendships can easily form, and just as easily dissolve. They lack the staying power of firm, solid friendships.

On the opposite side of the spectrum are friendships of *character*. In these relationships, we wish the well-being of our friend for his or her own sake. Our love for the Good is what draws us together and keeps us united through thick and thin. Becoming good by living the virtuous life is the common motivation. Once forged, such friendships do not dwindle or fade. They last a lifetime.

Aristotle goes on to provide three characteristics of true friendships: (1) benevolence, whereby we not only wish our friends well, but also actually seek their well-being; (2) reciprocity, which insists on a mutual rapport between friends and warns of the dangers of one-sided relationships, and (3) mutual indwelling, which enables each friend to see himself or herself reflected in the other as another self.[11]

Because of their coherency and near-universal appeal, these insights have often been used by theologians to shed light on the meaning of Christian friendship. Thomas Aquinas, the great thirteenth-century Dominican theologian, for example, says that charity is like "a certain friendship with God" and contains each of these important characteristics.[12] A person who is a friend of God shares an intimate relationship with him and lives a life of charity. To be a friend of God is to share in the inner life of God, to participate in the benevolent, reciprocal, and mutually indwelling love of the Trinity itself.

Contemporary authors say much the same. In her recent book, *She Who Is*, theologian Elizabeth Johnson uses the concept of friendship as a way of explaining of the relations within the Trinity:

> The mutuality experienced in genuine friendship offers one fertile clue into how to characterize the relations in the Trinity. Friendship is the most free, the least possessive, the most mutual of relationships, able to cross social barriers in genuine reciprocal regard. Like all good relations friendship is characterized by mutual trust in the reliability of the other(s), but what makes it unique is that friends are fundamentally side-by-side in common interests, common delights, shared responsibilities."[13]

She goes on to describe human friendship as an imperfect, but genuine, reflection of the love of the Trinity. Created in the image of God, the relations we form reveal something of the relations in the Godhead.

Christianity, one might say, proposes a threefold order of friendship. First, there is the community of friends in the Godhead itself: Father, Son, and Spirit are bonded together by their love of what is One, Good, True, and Beautiful. All seek each other's well-being, reciprocate their love for one another, and mutually indwell each other in an intimate embrace of love. Then, there is the individual's friendship with God. The same three characteristics resonate in my relationship with the ground of my being. We nurture a close, mutual rapport with one another: God seeks my well-being, and I seek God's; God dwells in me, and I dwell in God. Finally, there is friendship among Christians. United by their common interest in and friendship with God, Christians forge genuine bonds of friendship that enable them constantly to seek each other's interest in a respectful, reciprocal manner, in the hope of become a reflection of the other's love for God. All of these orders, moreover, interrelate. The befriending God fosters befriending Christians, who live in turn for the purpose of fostering an ever-widening circle of God's friends. In this respect, Christian friendship is one of the most precious treasures a person can be given. The scriptures agree:"A faithful friend is a sturdy shelter" (Sir 6:14). "There is a friend who sticks closer than a brother" (Prv 18:24). "A man can have no greater love than to lay down his life for his friends" (Jn 15:13).

Friends for the Journey

Where do such friendships come from? How are they formed? What is their purpose? Of all the possible answers, the one most difficult to prove is also the one that most captures the imagination: it is God who provides us with our friends for the journey; it is God's providential care for us which brings us into contact with those people with whom we freely choose to blaze our solitary trails through life.

In his book *Spiritual Friendship,* Aelred of Rievaulx, a twelfth-century Cistercian monk outlines four qualities of a genuine, God-centered friendship: love, affection, security, and happiness.[14] Love, for Aelred, means being there for our friends when they need us and showing our concern for their well-being. Affection means revealing our inward feelings in outward signs and gestures. Security is an atmosphere of trust that enables us to reveal our innermost thoughts without fear and suspicion. Happiness enables us to share everything with our friends: the good, the bad, and the ugly. These four qualities are present wherever God is the common interest that forges genuine bonds of human friendship. They are present in all true spiritual friendships, especially in those that bear the name "Christian."

These characteristics may seem idealistic, out-of-touch, or unrealizable in the humdrum of modern existence. Perhaps they are. But perhaps that is part of the problem: we have lost touch with the great art of making friends; we are too busy. Perhaps the words of the fox in Antoine de Saint-Exupery's *The Little Prince* have sadly come to pass: "Men have no more time to understand anything. They buy things all ready made at the shops. But there is no shop anywhere where one can buy friendship, and so men have no friends anymore."[15]

A spiritual friendship does not simply happen. It is hard work. It requires a long process of discernment. Later in his treatise, Aelred outlines four stages by which one enters into friendship with another: selection, probation, admission, and union.[16] As far as selection is concerned, he wonders why we hesitate when it comes to selecting our friends, when we are so good at selecting just about every other necessity of life. It is, however, something we must do: since not everyone is worthy of our trust, we should subject a person to intense scrutiny before we decide to go any further.

The second stage, that of probation, involves a process of building up a sense of mutual trust so that four essential qualities can be tested: (1) loyalty, whereby a person learns to trust his or her friend securely; (2) right intention, whereby a person's friend comes to expect nothing from the friendship but God and the natural good of the friendship; (3) discretion, whereby a person learns when to encourage and when to correct a friend; and (4) patience, whereby a friend learns not to bear hard feelings when confronted and to bear every adversity for the sake of the other.

In the third stage, that of admission, we finally recognize that we have become friends, and we refer to each other as such. It is here where we have to speak of different levels of friendship. Aelred himself recognizes a movement from being an acquaintance, to a companion, to a friend, to the most cherished of friends. Perhaps each of us should ask, "What are the different levels of friendships in my life? Who are my acquaintances? Who are my companions? My friends? My most cherished friends? The fourth stage, that of union, is perfect harmony in all things. Here, the friend becomes another self: "a single soul in two bodies." What happens to one's friend happens to oneself. That bond cannot be broken.

Becoming friends involves a long, arduous process: it takes a lot of time and energy, a lot of prayer and a recognition that God's hand is somehow at work in the circumstances of our lives. And then, at some point in the journey, a peculiar thing happens! While we are busy drawing close to our companions for our long walk through life, we gradually find that, all the while, God has been a present, silent partner in all we have done. As the Creator of all things, God is fascinated by all things and wishes to befriend anyone who shares in his many and varied interests—including roller coasters! He is a quiet unpretentious partner in all genuine human friendships. Were it not for him, there would be no stamps to collect, or flowers to garden, or roller coasters to ride. By merely keeping such things in existence, or allowing them to occur, he makes possible even the smallest gathering of friends—even a mere two or three.

For the most part, God is content with playing a supporting role in the development of such wholesome human friendships. Among his many interests, one in particular must be watching people become good friends. And given the great numbers of friendships formed today and throughout history, we can conclude that it is something he gets to do often.

As friendships deepen, it is not uncommon for people to become more and more aware of the presence of this silent third party. This unobtrusive partner will never bully his way onto center stage (God, after all, is just as absorbed as the friends themselves in the interest that binds them together). He must be invited. Only then will he come out of his position as a silent spectator and take a more prominent role in a relationship of friends. For some friends, this may amount to nothing more than the tacit recognition that their common interest or activity holds something of transcendent value. Others will sense a personal presence in the silence that forms the backdrop of their common activity. Still others will try to name it and, in doing so, come to a deeper recognition of the elusive nature of this silent prayer. By befriending that silence, friends embrace God himself as the source of their common interest and ground of their friendship. At such a moment, the friendship itself is consciously focused on God and merits to have the modifier "spiritual" placed before it.

Conclusion

What are we to conclude from all of this? In the words of one prominent turn-of-the-century Christian author:

> We ought to make more of our Christian friendships, the communion of the saints, the fellowship of believers. . . . What mutual comfort, and renewed hope, we would get from, and give to, each other! Faith can be increased, and love stimulated, and enthusiasm revived. The supreme friendship with Christ will not take from us any of our treasured intimacies. It will increase the number of them, and the true force of them. It will link us on to all who love the same Lord in sincerity and truth. It will open our heart to the world that Jesus loves and gave His life to save.[17]

St. Aelred himself could not have said it better.

Yes, the moment we are born, each of us begins a long walk through life, a journey that is full of surprises, unexpected twists and turns, unknown joys and sorrows. Each of us has been given certain friends for the journey. They are not there by accident. Some of them we already know and have known for many years. Others we have not yet met, and perhaps will not for some time to come. Let us thank the Lord for the gift of our friends. May the circle grow ever wider. May they continue to walk with us to our final destination. May we see in them a reflection of God's love for us and for the world which, this very moment, he holds in the palm of his hand.

Travel Questions

1. Are the people in your life just superficial acquaintances, "loose ties," who do not really matter to you—or you to them?

2. Are there any people in your life whom you would like to get to know better? What concrete steps could you take to do so? Are you willing to take the risk of befriending them? Do they mean enough to you that you are willing to put up with possible rejection?

3. Who are your close friends? How did you meet them? Why do you call them close friends? Do you find that some are closer than others? Have you ever lost the love of a close friend?

4. Who are people in your life with whom you can freely share and discuss your life of faith? How did these spiritual friendships come about? Did they take a long time to develop and mature?

5. Do you consider God your deepest and most intimate friend? Do you talk to God as you would a friend? Do you listen to God as you would a friend? Do you experience benevolence, reciprocity, and mutual indwelling in your relationship with God?

PASSIONATE PRAYER

Christ cannot love without feeling
and without heart. His love is human
as well as divine, and our charity will
be a caricature of his love if it
pretends to be divine only and does
not consent to be human.

—Thomas Merton,
No Man Is An Island[1]

Our closest companion on our journey through life is Christ himself. He travels before us to prepare our way; with us, to encourage us with each and every step; and behind us, to catch us when we tire and fall behind. He is so close, in fact, that we sometimes have a difficult time recognizing his presence in our midst. And even if we do, many of us have difficulty relating to him. For one reason or another, many of us insist on speaking to Christ in a very formal, cerebral sort of way. We hide from him our deepest thoughts and feelings: in part, because we are afraid of how he would react; in part, because we have somehow convinced ourselves that he does not care about what we really think and feel. Nothing, of course, could be further from the truth. On this leg of our journey, we look at the way we relate to our closest companion, friend, and guide. The more freely we find ourselves speaking and listening to him, the more easily we will be able to bear whatever hardships come our way on our long journey homeward.

Hidden Mistrust

Emotions are integral to our daily lives but, often enough, do not figure greatly in the way we pray. Because the way we *feel* is such a private—some might say secret— part of our personal makeup, many of us will go to great lengths to avoid sharing them with others, including God. Maybe this is because we do not feel at home with our emotions. Instead of cherishing them as an integral part of our being human, we experience them as wild and unruly forces that, if left unchecked, can easily overpower both reason and will, and lead us to do what we do not want to do (cf. Rom 7:15). As a result, we ignore them, control them, or, worst of all, repress them, thoroughly convinced all along that they have no particular significance for our spiritual lives. Such a conclusion could not be further from the truth. Affections play an important role in all authentic human relationships and should also figure greatly in our relationship with God. When they do not, something in our own self-understanding, or perhaps in our understanding of who God is, has gone terribly awry.

This dilemma is not an uncommon experience among people at prayer. Although most of us do not have much difficulty communicating our thoughts and intentions to other people, or to God, for that matter, we nevertheless find ourselves greatly inhibited when it comes to sharing our feelings. Part of the reason for this puzzling contrast may be that our ideas and aspirations come from what we have come to think of as the noblest powers of the human person: reason and the will. Our emotions, on the other hand, arise from what we think of as a less dignified source: the instinctual, animal side of our nature, the sensitive appetites. This latent mistrust of our concupiscent and irascible emotions implies a proportionate lack of trust in our bodily existence.

The Risk of Sharing

Try as we may to convince ourselves otherwise, most of us possess a subtle disdain for our physical existence that influences many of our thought patterns and social behaviors. We distrust our raw animal instincts because they bring us face to face with the limitations of our bodily natures and remind us of how much we have in common with the rest of the animal world. This distrust of our bodies is closely connected to the way we deal with our emotions. We do not want to manifest our feelings to others, because we are afraid of exposing the passionate, vulnerable side of our lives, that part of us over which we have the least control. Doing so involves a certain amount of risk that most of us are unwilling to take. Motivated by the fear of rejection and possible ridicule, we cover up our emotions with layers of sophisticated rational reflection. Since we feel awkward and, at times, even ashamed of our feelings, we clothe them in much the same way that we do our naked bodies, and, as we have been taught very early in life, we reveal them only to those who have earned our trust.

Sharing our feelings with others means that we believe in them enough to reveal the chaotic, messy side of our lives. It means that we feel comfortable enough with them to let down our guard and disclose a bit of our secret, inner lives, the part that we keep very close to the heart and allow only a few very close friends to see. A relationship of trust always involves a certain element of risk. Sharing our feelings and emotions means opening up the privacy of our hearts and stepping out in faith. We are never quite sure how our attempts at intimacy will be received; the possibility always exists that we will be ill-received, mistreated, or misunderstood. Taking that risk involves no small amount of courage, especially when a person is stepping out for the first time. It means going out on a limb and allowing others to see us as we really are.

God at Risk

What holds true for our dealings with other people applies equally well to our relationship with God. We relate to God through prayer: with it, we are able to draw near to God and grow in the spiritual life; without it, we have nothing but our own meager natural resources to help us find our way. St. Alphonsus Liguori puts the matter bluntly: "He who prays is certainly saved. He who prays not is certainly damned."[2] Whether we pray or not is a matter of life and death. Communing with God is as essential to our spiritual lives as air is to our natural, bodily well being.

The way we pray tells us as much about ourselves as it does of our image of God, and perhaps more. Although the forms of Christian prayer are many and varied, few would deny the importance of relating to God with our whole being: body, soul, and spirit (cf. 1 Th 5:23). Most of us realize that these dimensions of human existence form an integral unity that makes us unique in all of God's creation. "You shall love the Lord your God with all your heart, with all your soul, with all your mind, and with all your strength" (Mk 12:30). Jesus himself reminds us that we should hold nothing back in our love for God. To do so would evidence a lack of trust in the very God through whom "we live and move and have our being" (Acts 17:28). It would also indicate that there is a part of us that we are unwilling to turn over to the scrutiny of the divine gaze.

Why is it then that so many of us are hesitant to express our deepest feelings and emotions to God when we pray? Do we think that God is not interested in the various passions and affections that move us? Or is it because we ourselves do not see their relevance to our spiritual lives? Are we afraid of telling God how we really feel, afraid that God will see what we are really like and then no longer love us? The words of Yahweh to the prophet Jeremiah have something to tell us in this regard: "Before I formed you in the womb I knew you" (Jer 1:5). Whatever reasons may motivate us when we pray, we cannot get away from the simple truth that God already knows us through and through, better than we know ourselves. God knows our strengths and our weaknesses, our good points and our bad, our successes and our failures, our deepest hopes and our deepest afflictions. We should express everything within our hearts to God when we pray, not for God's benefit, but for our own.

Doing so manifests our implicit trust in God's presence in our lives. It shows that we are willing to keep nothing back from God, and that we desire the divine presence in every area of our lives—even in those things that embarrass us and of which we are ashamed. Not to do so shows that, for all our pious words and even good intentions, there is still a part of our lives, however small, that we are not yet quite willing to entrust to God. We do not yet fully believe in God's unconditional love for us. We believe that there is a part of us that God would shrug away from in disgust. And so we hide; we cover ourselves like our first parents after they ate from the tree of knowledge (Gn 3:7).

"You duped me, O Lord, and I let myself be duped. . . . All the day I am an object of laughter; everyone mocks me. . . . The word of the Lord has brought me derision and reproach all the day" (Jer 20:7–8). These words of Jeremiah to Yahweh give us an insight into the prayer of someone who holds nothing back from God. Here the prophet cries out to God out of anger at the circumstances in which he finds himself. He has responded to God's call and spoken God's words to his people only to be rebuffed and ridiculed. Now, he lets everything out in his prayer. All of his anger and frustration, his thwarted hopes and ambitions spill out from his heart and are voiced in the form of a complaint to God. Jeremiah prays in this way because of his utter confidence in God's activity in his life. He feels betrayed and quite alone, but he is still utterly convinced that his prayer will be heard and that his words—even those of complaint—will not go unanswered.

Jeremiah's passionate words reveal his intimate relationship with God. He is able to pray this way only because he feels a close rapport with God, a rapport that allows him to argue with God, to reveal his deepest sorrows and pains, to tell God off, even to curse God and to blame God for his misfortunes. The startling lamentations of Jeremiah remind us of the kind of intimacy with God we can experience on our journey. By holding nothing back from God, we slowly come to realize that God, all the while, has not been holding anything back from us. God is with us always, in the good times, as well as the difficult and lonely ones.

The Passionate God

One of the fundamental beliefs of the Christian faith is that Jesus Christ is the fullness of God's revelation to humanity. Most of us cannot appreciate the depth and meaning of this statement, because we have been trained to look upon revelation in terms of dogmatic truths rather than as God's personal self-disclosure to humanity. With the latter approach, however, the statement assumes much more profound significance, one that includes the notion of revelation as content, but goes far beyond it. To say that Jesus of Nazareth represents the fullness of God's revelation means that God has chosen to manifest the depths of the divine love in the person of Jesus. God has entered into human experience and given us in the person of Jesus a decisive glimpse into the divine nature. In doing so, humanity now has the potential to experience God from the inside out, just as God now experiences humanity.

The mystery of the Incarnation speaks of a divine love that is so ready and willing to communicate with its creation that it actually becomes one of us in order to help us to understand more fully who and what it is. "The Word became flesh and made his dwelling among us" (Jn 1:14). God holds nothing back in Jesus Christ: by becoming one of us, God reveals the compassionate depths of the divine nature; by dying for us on the cross, God manifests to us the extent of the divine love; by becoming bread and wine for us, God provides us with spiritual food for our long journey through life; by rising from the dead, God keeps alive in us the hope that every part of us will one day be transformed. God has entered our world and loved us completely, to the point of dying for us, becoming our spiritual nourishment and the source of our hope. In the person of Jesus Christ, God manifests to us the depths of the divine compassion as someone loves us unconditionally and who holds nothing back from us.

The reason that we can feel free to express ourselves fully to God is that Jesus Christ has already manifested the height, breadth, and depth of God's love for us: "Though he was in the form of God, he did not deem equality with God something to be grasped at" (Phil 2:6). The Word of God has no need to hold itself back or to keep a reserved place at God's right hand; it comes to us freely, because of its intense listening to the Father's perception of our own human needs. "Rather, he emptied himself and took the form of a slave" (Phil 2:7). The Word of God pours itself out into our human estate so that it can experience what it means to be human and, in doing so, be able to understand our human situation from where we are. God not only *understands* our feelings and emotions, but has even *felt* them in the person of Jesus Christ, who has become like us in all things but sin (cf. Heb 4:15).

Passionate Prayer

"God became human in order that humanity might become divine."[3] This well-known soteriological principle gives us another important insight into the relationship between Jesus, the Word made flesh, and the life of prayer. If it is true that God became human so that we might become divinized and thus able to share more deeply in the life of the Trinity, it follows that *all* that makes us human will be transformed in that process, even the affective side of our nature. This work of healing and elevation will be accomplished in us by the movement of God's Spirit as we "groan inwardly while we await the redemption of our bodies" (Rom 8:23). Moved by the Spirit, that inward yearning for God makes us cry out in prayer "Abba, Father" (cf. Rom 8:15) and is a concrete sign that God's work of redemption is taking place in us.

When seen in this light, prayer becomes what St. Alphonsus Liguori refers to as the "necessary and certain means of obtaining salvation." Everyone receives sufficient grace to pray. If we cooperate with that grace, the work of redemption is sure to take effect in us. If we do not, we are surely lost.[4] Our prayers, one might say, are the concrete means that God uses to divinize every dimension of our beings: spirit, soul, and body.

We are called to orient every aspect of our lives, every element of who we are toward God's divine love. That means that our prayers must be spiritual, mental, physical, social, and, yes, even passionate. By bringing our emotions to God in prayer, we open up yet another dimension of our lives to the influence of the divine grace. By opening our passions up to the divine mystery, God is able to enter our own personal worlds ever more deeply and love us in such a way so as to nourish us and encourage us at every stage of our journey.

Praying in such a way brings our reciprocal relationship with God to the fore. Each of us is invited to enter into an active, personal friendship with the divinity, one that involves sharing the deepest and most intimate dimensions of our lives. The fact that God already knows everything there is to know about us does not diminish the importance of our open and voluntary sharing of self at this most personal of levels. Knowing something about someone is not the same thing as having that person voluntarily share it. A relationship of friendship involves a reciprocal "give and take" that can come about only when two persons break open the bread of their lives and share it with each other.

God has entered our world so that we might become divine. Jesus breaks bread with us and, in doing so, invites us to sit at table with his divine companions and to open our lives up to them. Sharing our feelings with God demonstrates our desire for intimacy with the divine: it shows that we take the call to divine friendship seriously, and it manifests our desire to open every aspect of our lives to the influence of God's healing and elevating grace. By directing our passions to God, we enrich and ennoble them and demonstrate our desire to integrate them fully into our lives. Only through God's grace at work in us will our disordered affections one day be made whole; only by turning them over to God will we ever be released from their life-threatening stranglehold and freed to love God with all our heart, soul, mind and strength.

Conclusion

Passionate prayer is ultimately a request for conversion. In prayer of this kind, we beg God to enter into the emotional circumstances of our lives and to do in us what we are incapable of doing ourselves. A prayer of passion comes from the heart; it seeks to make sense out of our affections in light of God's unconditional love for us. By listening to our feelings, and then expressing them to God, we reveal not only our confidence in the divine friendship, but also our deep-rooted desire for a complete change of heart. "Convert us Lord and we will be converted" (Lam 5:21). By sharing with God our sadness and our joys, our anger and our pain, our longings and our hopes, we give God an open invitation to work some quiet miracles in our lives. We ask God to transform our unholy passions into holy ones so that we will gradually be more and more able to understand the height, breadth, and depth of the divine passion for us. In this way we hope to respond more generously to the promptings of the Spirit that come to us at every turn in our journey.

Travel Questions

1. How would you describe your prayer life to another person? Do you pray every day? Many times a day? Hardly at all? Almost never? Do you pray with all of your being, i.e., with body, soul, and spirit? Do you ever pray with others? Do you favor one form of prayer over another?

2. How do your emotions fit into your life of prayer? Do you reveal them freely to God? Sometimes? All of the time? Hardly ever? Do you feel that you have to hide them from God? Do you think that God is not concerned with them?

3. What most holds you back from sharing your feelings with God? Do you yourself place any importance in them? Are

you embarrassed by them? Do you think of them as unruly forces that must be carefully checked lest they get out of hand?

4. Do you know your own feelings? Are you able to distinguish them and name them? Do you reflect on them? Do you ever share them with others? When was the last time you had a heart-to-heart talk with another person?

5. Do you really believe that, in Jesus, God has experienced the fullness of human emotion? Do you really believe that Jesus revealed to us the compassionate face of God? How would you describe your feelings toward God? How would you describe God's feelings toward you?

CALLED TO COMMUNITY

Apostles of the hidden sun
Are come unto the room of breath
Hung with the banging blinds of death,
The body twelve, the spirit one,
Far as the eye, in earth arrayed,
The night shining, the supper laid.

—Oscar Williams
"The Last Supper"[1]

We find support for the successful completion of our journey not only in friendship and prayer, but in community life. Community is an intrinsic element of the call to discipleship; it offers us membership in a living fellowship of faith and helps to mediate our spiritual and moral concerns to the wider world.

Statements such as these normally elicit little disagreement and little controversy. Whatever our particular calling in life, most of us recognize the importance of some kind of community to support us in our journey of faith. Simple agreement, however, does not always evoke profound understanding; it may even keep us from taking a deeper look at the meaning of our closest assumptions. How many of us, for example, understand our call to community as something at the very center of our response to God? How many of us think of life in community as something intrinsic to our relationship to God, as something that actually leads us more deeply into the mystery of who God is? And how many of us actually avert to these ideas in the day-to-day circumstances of our lives? On this leg of our journey, reflection on the nature of our call to community will enhance the vision of our vocation to discipleship and how it is to be lived out in daily practice.

Vision and Call

Everyone needs a vision in life. Call it a dream, a purpose, a founding myth, or a narrative of origins; whatever you call it, we all need something in our lives to help us make sense out of our experience and to give us a way of sharing it with others. One of the purposes of Christian community is to keep such a vision in the forefront of our concerns and to encourage us to take concrete steps to pursue it in our everyday lives. It does so by reminding us of the larger context of our lives and by keeping us in touch with the traditions that have shaped us. It also does so by challenging us to confront the dark side of our human experience and to remain steadfast in our response to God's call in our lives.

Communities come in different sizes and shapes because they respond to different needs within the church and reflect the vast variety of God's creation. Families and base communities, parishes and religious congregations, secular institutes and third-order sodalities all exist for a purpose and flourish when they respond well to the needs they seek to fulfill.

Community is not something peripheral to God's call, as if its purpose was only to provide a conducive atmosphere to private personal spiritual growth or to respond to a pressing need in the structure of our anthropological makeup. Christian community can and does provide for such things. It is meant, however, to be and to do so much more. Life in community is intrinsically related to our journey into the mystery of God; it is part and parcel of our Christian vocation. Christian community loses its sense of purpose and conviction when it is taken out of the context of a call. Christian vocation seeks to enter more deeply into the divine mystery and is hence inherently communal. It is impossible to have one without the other.

By *vocation*, I am referring here not to the more qualified sense of the term as a specific state in life in the church (i.e., religious, priestly, or lay), but to the underlying call to intimate friendship that God extends to everyone, believer and non-believer alike. This call to beatitude—or the "beatific vision" as previous generations of theologians have referred to it—extends to all people, regardless of their faith, nationality, race, or position in life. It underscores the capacity all of us have to be lifted up through the influence of grace and to see God face to face. This mystical vocation which all of us share is nurtured and forged through life in community. Because God's nature is inherently communal, our call to divine friendship is worked out and perfected through a life lived with and oriented toward others.

The Trinitarian Community

The Christian tradition acclaims God as the perfect community of love. God who has conceived of us, who has created us, and who holds us in being, relates to us in a manner proportionate to his nature. God, who is love, relates to us in love, and cannot do otherwise. This is not the place to expound the vast intricacies of the doctrine of the Trinity. Suffice it to say that, however we describe this mystery of intimate social relations, be it through the traditional formulation of Father/Son/Spirit, or more recent innovations such as Creator/Redeemer/Sanctifier or Ground/Other/Bond, the mutual indwelling of persons must somehow be understood as occurring in the very nature of the Godhead. Although the mystery of God is inexhaustible and no single formulation can fully convey its meaning and depth, revelation teaches us that God is communal by nature, a single being of three clearly differentiated relations. When viewed in this manner, union with God becomes for us a never ending journey into the intimate community of divine relationships.

All of this may sound rather abstract and unrelated to the daily concerns of life in Christian community. Lofty ideas about the Trinity may seem to have little practical value when it comes to the nitty-gritty tensions and concerns of communal living. We should not forget, however, that the Trinity rests at the summit of the hierarchy of truths and, when all is said and done, is really the ultimate reality from which all else flows. The Trinity is *the* quintessential fact. It is not simply a metaphor, or a purely human construct, or a projection of our deepest hopes onto a divine plane. It is an element of God's self-disclosure to humanity which, in its doctrinal formulation, has the status of an divinely revealed truth. In this respect, the intimate community who is God and whom we call the Trinity is the beginning and end, the alpha and omega, of all things. It is the goal toward which we tend, the force that directs our lifelong activity, the reality that draws us to our final destiny.

Life in Christian community is the primary way in which God prepares us to participate in the mystery of tri-une love. If it is true, as St. Augustine and many of the medievals thought, that God has left traces or vestiges of the divine nature imprinted in the fabric of creation, then one may point to life in Christian community as an important instance where a person can discover a reflection of God's hidden presence in the world. Whenever we participate in community, we are really experiencing a vestige of God's triune love.

It would be presumptuous to expect that any of us would be willing or even able to share in the intimate relations of the divine nature without a long period of preparation. Most of us will need to be led, step by step, along the long and narrow way of the Lord. Christian community, one might say, is the fiery forge in which God tempers our personalities and gets them ready to share more deeply in the fullness of the divine community. It stretches our character and challenges us to live lives that increasingly take others into account. To use an example from the mystical tradition, it *purges* us of our imperfections, *illumines* us along our journey through life, and eventually brings us to a state of *union* with God. Life in community helps us to discover and become our truest, deepest selves; it naturally overflows in our relationship with others; and it shows us precisely what it means to be friends of God. The more deeply we enter into it, the more we prepare ourselves for our relationship with God both now and in the life to come. Such is the role of Christian community, that fellowship of God's friends, otherwise known as *koinonia* that we call "church."

The Way of Jesus

If the trinitarian basis of Christian community is still too abstract a notion to give us practical guidance in day-to-day living, a more concrete example comes from the life of Jesus himself. A careful reading of the gospels shows that he was always calling people to fellowship, especially those who were outcasts from the respectable social enclaves of his day. Prostitutes and tax collectors, the poor and the possessed, the blind and the lame were all welcomed by him and invited to partake in the friendship he shared with the Father. His gathering of disciples, his preaching through parables, his emphasis on table fellowship, his institution of the eucharist in the context of a meal: all reveal his deep concern to provide others with a sense of God's gratuitous love and care for them. Jesus reached out to others simply because they were children of the Father, and they were in need of God's friendship. He needed no other reason to call us his friends (Jn 15:15).

Jesus' call to fellowship continues to this day. Then, as now, fellowship is the perfect expression of the Son's intimate love of the Father. His fourfold movement of: (1) entering our world (in the incarnation), (2) giving of himself completely (to the point of dying for us), (3) becoming our very food and nourishment (in the eucharist), and (4) being the source of our hope (in the resurrection) is a concrete expression of the same selfless giving that characterizes the divine trinitarian relations. Jesus' love for humanity reveals to us an even deeper love which he shares with his Father. This intimate relationship enables him to listen to the Father's concerns as a loyal and faithful Son. His humble response manifests the self-diffusive nature of God's love and discloses the underlying reason for the entire Christ event.

Jesus' life provides us with an ideal vision of what life in community should be. Just as Christ entered our world and gave of himself completely to the point of becoming nourishment and a source of hope for us, so too are we called, both individually and communally, to enter the various worlds of people around us and give ourselves to them in a manner commensurate to that of Christ's sacrificial offering of self, to the point that we too become nourishment for them and a source of life-giving hope.

This calling reveals to us the fundamental meaning of our Christian identity. It is accomplished, not by ourselves alone, but as we cooperate with Christ working in us and influencing us by the grace of his Spirit. As might be expected, it is in the eucharist where this process of divinization takes on its most concrete and visible form. There, we gather as "church" around the table of the Lord and pray to the Father, through the Son and in the Spirit. There, we celebrate the fellowship of God's friends by reenacting the close ties between Jesus' last meal on earth and his sacrificial death the following day. There, we welcome the presence of the risen Lord not only in our hearts and in our midst, but in the very food we eat and drink. There, we celebrate the gift of "God among us" and recognize, in the breaking of the bread, that we also are called to become christs.

Practical Realities

These trinitarian and christological bases for life in community should not obscure the many obstacles which get in the way of our growth in the Spirit. The vision of what we can become and of what we are called to live comes up time and time again against the fragile and often divided constitution of the human heart. As members of Christ's body, we recognize our divine calling to share in God's love and to carry on Christ's mission through time. We also recognize, however, that human limitations and purely self-centered concerns often prevent us from living up to our noble aspirations. Sin in its various constructs—original, social, personal—distracts us from our mission

and leads us into unholy compromises that ultimately fragment our vision and detach us from the practical realities
of daily life. What follows are ten of the most common difficulties faced by communities in their attempt to live out
the implications of their call.

1. *Lack of Vision.* It can appear as lack of faith, a refusal to
   delve beneath the surface of things, or an inability to see
   the close connection between the lives we live and the beliefs we espouse. Whatever form it takes, a Christian community can very easily get out of touch with its charism or
   very reason for existence. Vision is a matter of both head
   and heart. It is not enough to give minimal intellectual as-
   sent to the values and goals which originally called the particular community into existence. The vision must seize
   the imagination of the members and generate in them a
   desire to realize the objectives of their community in their
   present situation. For this reason, a Christian community is
   always in need of inspired dreamers who will keep the
   founding vision of the community in the forefront of the
   community's consciousness, and prudent leaders who are
   able to interpret this vision in the context of the practical
   exigencies of daily life. If the vision is not somehow kept
   alive, the community will lose its focus, dissipate its ener-
   gies, and eventually go out of existence.

2. *Dysfunctional Structures.* Every community needs structures to organize itself for its own good and the good of its
   members. Structures give the community a certain amount
   of stability and enable it to function over a long period of
   time with a recognizable degree of continuity. Structures
   can be both a blessing and a curse. If the community is not
   careful, its structures can lose their relevance over time and
   actually inhibit the ways in which its members relate.
   When this occurs, structures become dysfunctional and de-
   prive the community of the tranquillity it needs to carry
   out its life and stated tasks. For this reason, every community needs to examine its structures periodically with a
   view to changing those that are either no longer necessary

or that needlessly obstruct the lives of its members. Since there is only one perfect community, the Holy Trinity itself, communities should not be surprised to find a certain degree of dysfunctional relating in their internal structural organization. The goal here should be to minimize as far as possible the existence of harmful or irrelevant structures and to replace them with those that truly respond to the needs and goals of the community.

3. *Communal Introversion.* Communities need to interact with the world around them. If they cut themselves off from their surrounding environment and become overly concerned with their own internal affairs, they run the risk of losing touch with reality and their ability to make sound, prudent decisions. History is full of examples of communities which have followed this dangerous and often tragic course. Communities that engage in communal "navel gazing" become a world unto themselves and have a tendency to define themselves in terms of their opposition to the world from which they have cut themselves off. For this reason, a community's valid concern to define itself internally must be taken in stride and complemented with efforts to open itself to, dialogue with, and engage the world around them. The health of the community requires that its members extend their reach beyond its borders and offer hospitality and service to those in need.

The flip side of introversion is the danger of extroversion. In reaching outward, care must be taken not to fall into the opposite extreme. If it falls into extreme extroversion, a community becomes so absorbed in external activities that it loses touch with the inner life that propels it and gives its actions meaning.

4. *Tensions Between the Individual and Community.* One of the great strains in community life often has to do with the way the relationship between the community and its individual members is conceived of and carried out. When this issue is not constructively resolved, we often

find one of two unhealthy extremes developing: either the community demands complete and utter conformity of its members in the minutest details of their personal lives, even at the expense of an individual's psychological health and mental stability; or individual members gain so much autonomy over their lives that the claims made by the community become virtually non-existent, to the detriment of the community's social viability and corporate existence. Christian communities should try to strike a proper balance between these extremes by highlighting the complementary relationship between the individual and his or her corporate identity. In doing so, it will be able to emphasize the dignity of the human person in the context of the community environment which mediates the world to the individual and through which the individual responds.

5. *Personality Conflicts.* Community members can fit anywhere across a large spectrum of personality types. However these various types are conceived—be it according to Jungian categories or the Myers-Briggs nomenclature, or even the nine points of the enneagram—it is commonly agreed that a variety of personality types provides the community with a rich basis of human strengths and talents from which to draw and further its goals. Such variety, however, also has its drawbacks and liabilities, not the least of which is the great likelihood that certain personalities will conflict and become a disturbing factor in the life of the community. When such conflicts arise, those involved should be encouraged to look upon them as an opportunity for growth. Nowhere is it stated that community members have to be close confidants, intimate friends, or even that they have to like each other. They should, however, be able to surmount differences in outlook and taste for the common good of the community to which they belong. The witness offered by such selfless efforts should not be minimized. We who are exhorted by Christ to "love

our enemies" (Mt 5:43) should make a special effort to co-operate with and be kind to those members of our own communities with whom we do not get along.

6. *Questions of Intimacy.* Friendship is a gift from God and should be welcomed with special joy when it develops among members of a community. Close friends, however, should be aware of the responsibility they have to insure that their relationship is integrated into the life of the community and that their relationship is open to others. When this does not occur, friendship can become divisive and have a harmful effect on the life of a community (hence, at least part of the reason for the deep suspicion of particular friendships in the tradition of many religious communities). Friends who are members of the same community should be encouraged to reflect from time to time on the meaning of their relationship for the community. How are they contributing to the life of the community? In what ways are they detracting from its goals and purposes? Are they overly possessive of the time they spend with one another? Do they make room for others by making the effort to invite them to participate in their activities and reflections? Friends who ask such questions of themselves usually escape the danger of forming unhealthy cliques and can make a great contribution to the life of the community.

7. *Different Motivations.* Tensions also arise because members have joined the community and continue to belong to it for different reasons. Few of us are so constituted that we act entirely from pure and noble intentions. More often than not, we bring a host of other invisible but powerful motivating factors to the choices we make. These can range anywhere from troubled family histories to economic concerns, from educational interests to limited career choices, from deeply rooted psychological needs to a desire for an upwardly mobile social respectability. Community leaders must recognize the inevitability of such

mixed motivations, try to bring them to the surface of their members' consciousness, and work to minimize the effect of those which have are harmful to the life of the community. The more these mixed motivations are properly understood and dealt with, the easier it will be for members to grow beyond of them and to focus their energy on the motivating factors that are explicitly stated and professed by the community as a whole.

8. *Indifference.* Members need to feel that their contribution counts in the life of the community. If they do not feel this way, it will be very easy for them to dissociate themselves emotionally from the spirit of the group and manifest their disillusionment through non-committal, passive-aggressive behavior or, worse yet, sheer indifference. Apathy can arise for any number of reasons (e.g., dysfunctional structures, personality conflicts, personal difficulties). Whatever the reason, members who display a marked indifference to the life and goals of the community should be asked to explain their behavior. Often, indifferent behavior is a sign of some deeper issue that is not being addressed either by the individual or the group. If these deeper issues are not surfaced and appropriately addressed, the community runs the risk of letting more and more of its members succumb to the awkward and painful situation of deliberated uninvolvement. It is always better to deal with such situations before they get out of hand and influence the behavior of the entire community.

9. *Lack of Awareness.* Members can have all the good will in the world, but may simply not be aware of the particular needs of their community in a given situation. This lack of awareness may be due to their own lack of sensitivity to the needs of the group, to differing assumptions about the division of labor within the group, or to the failure of those responsible within the community to make these needs known.

   Awareness of the details of community living and the corresponding decision to get personally involved and do something about them can help to create an atmosphere of participation that will serve the community well. By nurturing a habit of awareness in the small details of community living, members will be well-equipped to be sensitive in larger, more significant situations down the road. Such awareness of details will help to insure the smooth running of the internal affairs of the community and contribute in important ways to the realization of its larger purposes and goals.

10. *Loneliness.* A certain degree of loneliness is to be expected in community life. Members need to cope with such feelings in ways that will lead them to a healthy integration of their experience. When this does not take place, community members can come to exist in near complete isolation from one another: they live and even work together, but rarely relate to one another on anything other than the most superficial of levels. Extreme bouts of loneliness among community members often represent an unwillingness on their part to delve beneath the surface of their lives and to share the experiences and concerns. Steps should therefore be taken in the community to build up an atmosphere of trust where members will feel free to relate some of the pain they experience in their personal lives and in the life of the community. Just how this is done will depend on the size of the community and the willingness of its members.

While Christian communities must never lose sight of the vision which calls them into being and sustains their continued existence, they must also deal with the practical, and often painful, realities of everyday life. Those able to integrate these two aspects of the same call will reach a deeper understanding of the nature of God's presence in human history and the way he continues to work and act in their midst. Those who do not do so run the risk of contributing to the downward spiral of repeated mistakes that ultimately leads to stagnation and loss of life.

Conclusions

The above discussion brings three important conclusions to the fore. In the first place, the call to community is not something peripheral to the Christian life, but an essential ingredient of our common journey into the mystery of God. An authentic Christian community must be sustained by a trinitarian and christological vision and, at the same time, be flexible enough to deal with the practical, everyday difficulties that will surely arise as it seeks to live out that vision. When the difficulties are overlooked, the community will either have unrealistic expectations of what it can do as a community; or, if the vision is lost, the community may simply give up trying to make it a better place to live. If both are kept in mind, the community is able to keep the vision before it, while also taking prudent steps for improving the quality of its life and witness.

In the second place, this twofold focus of vision and practical reality comes together in the life of the community through the call to conversion. Community members should be constantly reminded that there is only one *perfect* community, the Trinity itself. When they fail to live up to the vision which they profess, they should not get discouraged or depressed, but accept their failures as an invitation to change. Try as we may, few of us are capable of turning our lives around completely on our own efforts. We need the help of others to encourage us along the way and the grace of God to change our hearts and to fill us with a deep desire to conform our lives according to his will. The call to conversion brings together the vision of what we one day hope to become and the concrete reality of who and what we are. It highlights both facets of community and reminds us that, when all is said and done, change will come about only when we are docile to the Spirit and open to the initiative of God in our lives.

Finally, a community of conversion must, first and foremost, be a community of prayer. If a Christian community does not turn to God and ask for help in sustaining its vision and enabling it to cope with its shortcomings, if its members do not pray together and lift up each other's needs, if they do not ask the Lord to change their hearts and help them to overcome their weaknesses, then no amount of talking or planning or concerted action will do any good in bringing about substantial changes in the quality of its life and witness. If, on the other hand, community members pray together for the humility to accept the truth and to acknowledge their failures, if they ask for the courage to forgive those who have hurt them and to approach those whom they have hurt, if they ask God to make them generous with their time and open with their lives and willingness to share, then they will already be well on their way to experiencing the mystery of God befriending them where they are and helping them, as a group, to enter more deeply into the divine mystery. The call to community manifests itself as a call to conversion, which itself becomes a call to a deeper life of prayer. Prayer is the vehicle which carries us to our destiny in God. With it, there is nothing to fear and everything to hope for; without it, we lose sight of both the vision and the practical realities that promise to shape us and guide us along our journey homeward to intimate union with the divine.

Travel Questions

1. What types of communities have you belonged to during your life (e.g., family, parish, club, religious congregation)? Which did you like the best? Do you know why? Have you ever felt called to one community in particular? How did you respond to that call?

2. Has life in community been an important factor in your life as a Christian? Has it been a positive or a negative influence? Do you find it easy to live in community? What, in your opinion, makes community life a challenge?

3. Which of the ten practical realities of community life

resonate with your own experience? How did you cope with them in the past? Is there anything you would do differently? Which do you find most disturbing? Why?

4. Do you normally think of community as something intrinsically related to the call to discipleship? If so, how has your experience of community helped you to follow Jesus more closely? How has it impeded you in your life of discipleship?

5. Do you normally think of your life as a continuous journey into the depths of God's love? If so, then in what practical ways does this belief affect your daily life? How does it affect your thoughts about and prayers to God?

RE-IMAGINING GOD

Nothing so changeless as the changing sky;
Nothing so lonely as its purple arc;
Nothing but man so propped by mystery;
Nothing but life as swift from bright to dark;
Nothing so vast as this great heaven tree
Housing the whirlwind and the tremendous lark.

—Henry Morton Robinson,
"Heaven Tree"[1]

Our journey is swiftly drawing to a close. As we begin this final leg, we look back upon the road we have traveled and remember the wealth of experience that has led us homeward. Out of the dark side of hope, we have traversed the lonely expanses of the heart in our search of the innocence of lost childhood, struggling all the while to rise above the forces of self-deception that have distracted us along the way. We have also learned the importance of opening our hearts to others so that through the graces of friendship, prayer, and community life we might walk further along the road to conversion that will lead us to the Tavern at the End of the World, that place we call Home. For some time now, the way of the pilgrim has run parallel to and gradually merged with the way of the mystic. It should not surprise us then when we find references here and there to pilgrimage to as "the poor man's mysticism."[2] The two roads share a great deal in common—and for us have now become one.

In our search for holiness, God has beckoned us and guided us at every step. As we near our destination and look back on our pilgrim's way, it might be helpful for each of us to reflect upon how even our image of our Maker has changed during the course of our journey. The better we get to know someone, the more readily are we able to cast off any stereotypes of him or her that we have picked up along the way. The same is true of our relationship with God. He continues to elude our grasp even as our knowledge of him deepens.

Imagining God

I have believed in God for most of my life. I have believed in him for so long that it is hard for me to imagine what it would be like not to believe in him. The concept of God is so fundamental to my outlook on life that I could not survive long in this world without it. Doubts have come and gone, to be sure; some have even returned and made a home for themselves in my heart; others I have be-friended and now call by different names. I have doubted God's care for the world; I have doubted God's concern for me; I have, at times, even doubted God's existence. Of all my misgivings about my faith, the ones that I find most difficult to deal with are those having to do with the way I imagine or "image" God to be.

Most of us realize that God encompasses much more than the ideas and concepts we use to describe him. But how many of us allow such knowledge to take root in our hearts? How many of us have ever taken a good hard look at the images we have of God, the ones with staying power, those that inspire us and give us hope, as well as those that haunt us in our sleep and fill us with dread? How many of us have ever ventured beyond the safe stereotypes which we so often use to placate our modern sensibilities? To acknowledge God's existence is not the same as seeking him in faith. The Living God—the God of Abraham, Isaac, and Jacob—bids us not to worship our idea of him but to journey with him, to encounter him, and to wrestle with him in the most unexpected places of our everyday lives.

A God of Variety

If the story of creation (Gn 1:1-2:4) is anything to go on, God has not only a strong penchant for variety, but also a gloriously inventive imagination. Time and again, we find him calling forth all kinds of new, previously unthought of creations: darkness and light, water and land, the sun, the moon and the stars, sea monsters and swimming things, all sorts of birds, various beasts both wild and tame, man and woman. The scriptures depict God as someone in love with variety; the richness of creation is nothing but a reflection of God's interest in "all kinds of living things" (Gn 1:24). He gives the world not one kind of fish, bird, or animal, but hundreds, literally thousands upon thousands of species and sub-species. Nothing less

than a power of infinite imagination could concoct anything like the world in which we find ourselves.

God's love for variety tells us something about himself.
The Christian doctrine of the Trinity depicts a God whose
love for variety expresses itself in intimate unity, and, con-
versely, whose intimate unity is manifested in rich variety.
God is the perfect community of love who has brought all
things into existence and who sustains them with each passing moment. Only a God whose very nature exudes plurality would give us a world with such a great assortment of
creatures in it. And only he would place at the summit of his
creation people like ourselves who have a similar fascination
both for variety and the inventive impulses of the imagination. No wonder we resort to a variety of ways to imagine
who he is and the role he plays in our lives! Are we not made
in his own image and likeness? Would God himself expect
anything less of us?

Despite our vast creativeness, the images we use to describe God probably tell us more about ourselves than
him. God's plurality and unity are intimately and mysteriously tied: one cannot exist without the other. Our plurality, however, is dispersed and fragmented. We are a people
"out of sorts" with the world, with others, and with ourselves. Even our language, as rich and imaginative as it can
be, runs up against its inherent limitations. Try as we may,
the names we give God always fall short of our expectations.

We call God "Father" and yet somehow sense that he is
also "not Father," "more than Father"—and all of these
things simultaneously! The same can be said for "Son," and
"Spirit," as well as the many other names and attributes we
give God (e.g., Mother, Brother, Friend, Spouse, Ground,
etc.). Because of their inherent capacity both to reveal and
to obscure, our words reach beyond themselves and point
to a mystery that no language can ever fully capture. Try as
we may, we fail to come up with adequate ways to describe

our experience. Our words want, and yet we cannot get beyond them; they fail us, sometimes miserably, but still, they are important to us. When chosen wisely and with care, they transcend themselves and put us in touch with our deepest yearnings. Even though they pale before God's infinite majesty, they enable us to express what matters most to us and help us to get in touch of our deepest dreams and secretly guarded hopes.

The Varieties of God

At various times in my life, I have bowed my head to both true and false images of "God." These images arose out of many things: the way I was brought up, my early schooling, the demands of the moment, my state of mind at the time, and the particular mood I happen to be in. Too many to count, a short list of the more deeply rooted images should show how highly "charged" a simple word like "God" can become.

On the darker side, God has been for me (and, I am sure, for many others): (1) the uncompromising police man, who is constantly looking over my shoulder just waiting for me to make a mistake; (2) a vengeful judge, who enjoys watching me pay the price; (3) a frantic workaholic, who is too busy ruling the universe to have any time for me; (4) a smiling wimp, who is so non-confrontational that I could never displease or disappoint him in any way (so why bother?); and (5) an indifferent couch potato, who simply just doesn't care about the evil in the world (so why should I?).

On the brighter side, God has been, among other things: (1) a close friend to whom I can talk and who actually listens; (2) a loyal spouse, who loves me for myself, no matter what I do; (3) a loving parent, who disciplines me for my own good; (4) a dedicated teacher, who challenges me to grow; and (5) an adventurous explorer, who always shows me unknown paths to walk.

These are the images of God that accompany me. Some are false images, idols, that seek nothing but to fragment and further disperse the many dimensions of who I am; others are manifestations of the true God, who calls me out of my self to serve others humbly out of love for him. Some may even seem ambiguous, fundamentally true, but exaggerated to an extreme. However they are perceived, at one time or another, each of them—both the true and the false, the slightly warped and the badly disfigured—has taken hold of me, seized me, filled me with its spirit, and moved me to action. Let there be no mistake about it: who and what I am destined to become depends very much on the images of God operative in my mind.

Re-imagining God

Like me, many of us are in desperate need today of re-imagining the reality, role, presence, and movement of God in our lives. This holds true not only for many of the false images and metaphors, which obviously must be struck down and discarded, but also for many of the true images of God in our minds which for a variety of reasons no longer stir our hearts and inspire us to love.

How could such a situation have ever evolved? For one thing, our media-crazed world has flooded our minds with so many vying, illusory images that it has become increasingly difficult for us to tell when we are being told the truth and when we are being deceived. Everything is now up for grabs and open to question; image has become more important than substance; cleverness and facility with words pass for character and integrity; everyone is now thought to have a hidden agenda. Slowly but surely, a subtle cynicism has become systemic to the way we conduct our public discourse. Relativity reigns: the individual has become the measure of truth; opinion polls determine the impact of ideas. The media has become the message, and most of it, unfortunately, is not the good news it so often makes itself out to be.

The transference of these tendencies onto the religious sphere has, in many instances, already taken place. Many of us have mistaken the likenesses we have made of God for God himself. We have allowed our words and images to get in the way of God's gentle movement in our lives. We use concepts and images to contain rather than to reveal the wonderful mystery of God in our lives. The images have become stale and commonplace; they no longer evoke passion and feeling; they fail to capture our imagination. And because they have become flat, we mistakenly conclude that God has lost interest and no longer plays an active role in our daily affairs.

How can we re-imagine God in our lives? What must be done to recapture the sense of God's living presence in our midst? How do we go about creating a space for him that is not already preprogrammed by the images we have of him and by our own preconceived ideas about the way he should act? Although there are no easy answers to such basic questions, I would like to make three suggestions about how we can improve our awareness of God's living presence in our lives.

1. *Image Fasting.* Jesus once told his disciples that certain obstacles in the spiritual life can be dealt with only through much prayer and fasting (Mt 17:21). The traditional understanding of fasting—abstaining from food and nourishment for a specified period of time—can, I believe, be expanded to include a measured refraining from "image intake," i.e., an inordinate exposure to the various conscious and unconscious messages that come from the media.

Like the food we eat and the water we drink, too much or too little exposure to the controlling images of our consumer society can kill us. "Image fasting" means trying to strike a proper balance in our lives when it comes to the media. It means deciding to break the nasty habits that lead us to live unexamined lives and using the media as an instrument of growth rather than a weapon of mass destruction. There are all sorts of ways in which a person can discipline himself or herself along these lines: listening to the radio only at appropriate times; reducing one's hours before the TV; putting aside the newspaper every now and again; not going to the movies as often; spending less time at the mall, etc. Even though any one of these activities may be good, the cumulative effect of these and other activities on our day-to-day lives can be to numb our spiritual sensitivities and put us more and more out of touch with the deeper levels of the self.

"Image fasting" also means creating a space in our lives for silence by foregoing some of the luxuries of contemporary Western culture that enrich us materially but which can all too easily impoverish us spiritually. It means being aware of the desensitizing effects the media can have on our lives and the determination to do something about it. "Image fasting" can help to create the conditions for the possibility of a deeper awareness of God in our lives. It means cooperating with God's grace in such a way that we become responsible stewards of the vast technological resources at our disposal.

2. *Theological Reflection. A* second way in which we can help to create the conditions for a renewed understanding of the presence of God in our lives is theological reflection. Theologians tell us that there are different models of theological reflection—directive and non-directive; scriptural and experiential, etc.—and that all can be appropriately adapted to individual and group contexts. Regardless of their differences in method and approach, all of these models seek to interpret human experience in light of the revealed truths of the Christian faith. This, in fact, is precisely what makes the reflection "theological" as opposed to philosophical or humanistic.

Theological reflection on the images that influence the way we think and act can help us to see the important differences between emotional reaction and responsible action. When applied to the various images of God, it can enable us to see more clearly both the great variety of images of God which influence in our day-to-day activities and the great distance between the particular idea of God supported by any one of these particular images and the mystery of God himself. This distinction is an invaluable help for anyone seriously interested in making progress in the spiritual life. Through it, we learn not to control God by confining him to a particular image or idea of our own making (and which often is nothing more than a projection of our own needs and desires onto a divine plane). We are encouraged instead to allow our understanding of God to inhabit a wide variety of images and metaphors which, when taken in conjunction with one another, convey much more of the mystery of who and what he is than what any single one of them could possibly communicate on its own.

When done in a group context, as it normally should be done, theological reflection also helps us to articulate the operative communal paradigm that sets the agenda for the way that particular group envisions its task before God and in the church. The more a community becomes aware of this operative paradigm, the greater its chances will be of seeing its limitations, offering new, counterbalancing images with which to offset the perceived weaknesses, and thus making room for the mystery of God to seep in between the intervening overlay of concepts. Theological reflection, in other words, encourages the type of variety regarding our images of God that permits creative reasoning and imaginative expansion of the traditional ways in which we envision God working in our lives.

3. *Imageless Prayer.* A third suggestion for re-imagining the role of God in our lives has to do with the way we pray. Whether we admit it or not, most of us have somewhere lurking in the back of our minds a particular image or idea of God that serves as a focus for our attention. This point

of concentration concretizes the act of prayer for us in a way that makes us feel as though we are talking to someone who is listening to our pleas and who, we instinctively feel, will in some way respond. Ideally—and this is the great insight of Eastern Christian spirituality—that image will serve as a window to the beyond, an instrument that opens up another world to us and allow our spirits to commune with the Spirit of God in the depths of our hearts.

In a society, however, that has in recent decades become desensitized to images of all shapes and sizes, a measured dosage of imageless prayer may be more of an aid to steady spiritual growth. This kind of prayer can be done in any number of ways: by sitting still in a room, emptying one's mind of all words, thoughts, and images, and simply being still, by doing the same before the Blessed Sacrament, by allowing one's spirit to breathe between the words of a particular spoken prayer. However it is done, one ultimately seeks to be still, to allow God to work, and simply let him be God in one's life.

The benefits of this kind of prayer are manifold: (1) it enables us to move beyond the images—both true and false—that we have of God, thus enabling us to appreciate more thoroughly the unpredictable ways in which he works in our lives; (2) it gives us an appreciation of the important counterbalancing role played by apophatic, or "negative," theology in the church's tradition; (3) it awakens the mystical side of our personalities and encourages us to seek an experience of God in the quiet that can be found in the interior reaches of the human heart; (4) it enables us to go back to the true images that we have of God and to enjoy them for what they are: accurate but inadequate representations that point in the right direction to a God who ultimately dwells beyond the rules of analogy and rational comprehension; (5) it beckons us to begin a journey into the unknown that begins anew whenever we pray in that manner and which will bring us ever more deeply into the unknown mystery of who God is and what we shall become. Imageless prayer calls each one of us to befriend the darkness in which the images in our mind can be seen. It asks us to welcome that darkness in the hope of seeing a deeper, brighter light that burns beyond the rim of human consciousness and promises to guide us home.

These three suggestions have important implications for our own self-understanding. Re-imagining God requires a thorough re-examination of who we are and the way we relate to others in our lives. Since how we relate to God is largely a function of the ways we have learned to deal with other people, the same helps we use in bettering our understanding of God can be used, with appropriate adaptations, to help us better understand our families, friendships, and own inner workings. When directed toward others and ourselves, image fasting, theological reflection, and imageless prayer can help us to distance ourselves from whatever dysfunctional ways of relating we have adopted over the years. By striking down the rigid stereotypes we have of ourselves and others, and by giving us room to be ourselves and to treat others in the same way, they provide us with the necessary tools for creating strong, healthy relationships. As difficult as it may be, re-imagining God in our lives promises to heal the battered image of the self and to show us wholesome ways of relating to ourselves, others, as well as to God himself.

Conclusion

"God created man in his image: in the divine image he created him; male and female he created them" (Gn 1:27). Our ability to imagine the divine in our midst stands out as one of the great signs of our noble stature in God's creation. Bearing his image, we alone in all of God's creation have the wherewithal to reciprocate by creating an image of him. The great responsibility that goes along with this gift cannot be emphasized enough. The images we make of God have vast repercussions for just about everything we do in life: from the way we act, to the other relationships we form, to the way we view and understand ourselves. To be unaware of these images, to ignore them, or to disregard their importance in our lives weakens our ability to discern the true images from the false and thus lessens our capacity to respond to the hand of God in the ordinary circumstances of our lives.

Because we have so often heard that the most deeply ingrained images of God in our minds are the products of such knotty primordial forces as primary family experiences, early upbringing, and the way religion was first taught to us, we sometimes overlook the important role played by our own free wills. Many of us have come to believe that we are utterly determined by our past, that the false images of God that haunt us are too deeply rooted in our psyches to be rooted out or struck down. We cannot believe that we, even through much prayer and fasting, can replace those false images of God that lurk deep in the recesses of our minds with ones that correspond more to the truth. We do not trust our powers of imagination and fail to believe that God is ever calling us to re-imagine his revelation to us in such a way that it always remains a vibrant, life-giving source of spiritual nourishment.

And it is true that there *are* limits to what we can imagine about God. When all is said and done, there comes a time when we must let go of our imaginings and re-imaginings of God and permit him to enter our lives and surprise us by his gentle yet ever-elusive presence. To allow God to be God in our lives we must let go of our neatly packaged concepts and ideas of him; we must put aside our images and thoughts of who he is and what he has said to us, and we must release ourselves even from the desire to see him with that interior spiritual sense which all of us seem to possess. To let God be God in our lives we must continue our lonely walk down the darkened path of faith, a steep narrow road that holds few earthly consolations other than the unswerving conviction that we are being led by a light we cannot see and following a faint, barely audible voice that rises ever so softly and quietly in our hearts and leads us to the peace of the traveler's rest.

Travel Questions

1. What images come to mind when you think of God? Does any one in particular stand out from the rest? Are you comfortable with these images? Are there any you would like to change? If so, why? And what would you replace them with?

2. In what ways do you experience God as Father? As Mother? As Brother? As Friend? As Spouse? Is there a particular image of God that you have a difficult time accepting? Is the reason for the difficulty something inherent in the image itself? Or does it have more to do with your own system of values?

3. How has your image(s) of God changed over the years? Has this change been for better or for worse? Do you find yourself at times reverting to an image of God that was prevalent in your life during your earlier years? Did this have a beneficial or detrimental effect on your spiritual life?

4. Have you tried any of these suggestions for improving your awareness of God's presence in your life (i.e., image fasting, theological reflection, and imageless prayer)? Are you particularly put off by one or the other? If so, why? Can you think of any other helpful means of delving more deeply into the reality of God's presence in your life?

5. If you had to shed all but one image of God, which would you choose? How would you react if you were then asked to cast aside even it? Do you trust God enough to carry you beyond the limitations of human language? Beyond the confines of all human knowledge? Beyond life and death itself? Do you trust God enough to carry you in the midst of darkness, to the peace of the traveler's rest?

THE TRAVELER'S REST

Far have I come this day,
From there, beyond the ridge
As far as eye can see.
Every step, half taken,
Half left behind;
Every path not chosen—
Now lost in memory—
Brings my journey here.

Far have I come,
Through thicket and through fog,
Over mountain fastness,
In the mud and in the bog.
Far have I come—
A lonely traveler,
Foraging for rest
Beneath the restless sky.

Now my journey dwindles to a step,
As aching limbs and back,
Soreness of foot, each breath,
The pain of miles traveled,
And of miles yet to come,
The sweat—
All bid my bones
The peace of traveler's rest.

There, by the wayside,
My home will be this night—
With staff beside the fire
And head beneath the stars.
Silently the night will carry rest,
Until the darkness turns to dawn,
And the morning sun sheds its solitary light
Upon my chosen path.

Now, at this quiet hour,
When shadows cast no more
And darkness covers day,
I remember moments passing.
And think of moments yet to come—
Moments which speak of my journey,
Which dwindle to a breath
And bring my weariness rest.

Heavy the lid falls upon the eye,
As the mind returns to dreaming,
As the soul becomes the sky.
Asleep in sleep, I wander
Through a thousand journeys,
To a thousand wayside places,
To a thousand unknown destinations—
And a single rude awakening.

Life is a journey, as is death—
And man the traveler.
His every breath, a step;
His every step, the breath of a journey ended:
Night dwindles into dawn,
The day into dusk,
the journey into the traveler's rest,
The traveler into his final hour.

Notes

Departure: Secret Stars

1. C.S. Lewis, *The Discarded Image:An Introduction to Medieval and Renaissance Literature* (Cambridge: Cambridge University Press, 1971), 99.

The First Leg

1. *The Song of the Bird* (Garden City, N.Y.: Image Books, 1984), 88.
2. Walter M. Miller Jr., *A Canticle for Leibowitz* (New York: Lippincott, 1959; 7th Bantam reprint, New York: Bantam, 1980), 259 [page references are to reprint edition].
3. Patricia Hampl, *Virgin Time* (New York: Ballantine, 1992), 220-21.
4. Jean Giono, *The Man Who Planted Trees*, with an Afterword by Norma L. Goodrich (The Condé Nast Publications (*Vogue*), 1954; reprint, Chelsea, Vt.: Chelsea Green, 1985), 34 [page references are to reprint edition].
5. Ibid., 38-39.
6. Thomas Merton, *No Man Is an Island* (Garden City, N.Y.: Image Books, 1967), 32.
7. Myles Connolly, *Mr. Blue* (N.Y.: Macmillan, 1928; 16th Image reprint, Garden City, N.Y.: Image Books, 1954), 76 [page references are to reprint edition].

The Second Leg

1. *Joyce Kilmer's Anthology of Catholic Poets*, with a new Supplement by James Edward Tobin, revised ed. (Garden City, N.Y.: Image Books, 1955), 138.

The Third Leg

1. *The Portable Blake* (New York: The Viking Press, 1974), 88.
2. C.S. Lewis, *Out of the Silent Planet* (New York: Macmillan, 1965; first paperback ed.), 122.
3. Robert Fulghum, *Maybe (Maybe Not): Second Thoughts from a Secret Life* (New York: Villard, 1993), 7-8.
4. Ibid., 7.
5. Georges Bernanos, *The Diary of a Country Priest,* trans. Pamela Morris (New York: Macmillan, 1937; paperback edition, 1962), 150.
6. Thomas Merton, *No Man Is an Island* (Garden City, N.Y.: Image

Books, 1967; reprint of 1955 ed. by special arrangement with Harcourt, Brace and World, Inc.), 150.

7. Ibid., 155.

8. This translation by Witter Bynner is cited in *The New York Times Magazine* (September 18, 1994), 20.

The Fourth Leg

1. *As There As the Sky* (Whitby, Ontario: The Plowman, 1995), 13.

2. Fydor Dostoyevsky, *Crime and Punishment*, trans. Sidney Monas (New York/London: Signet, 1968), 73.

3. Ibid., 271.

4. Ibid., 463 [words of Svidrigailov to Raskolnikov].

5. Fyodor Dostoyevsky, *The Idiot*, trans. Henry and Olga Carlisle (New York/London: Signet, 1969), 162.

6. Dostoyevsky, *Crime and Punishment*, 406-7.

7. Ibid., 407.

8. Ibid., 505.

The Fifth Leg

1. *Selected Poems* (New York: Harcourt, Brace & World, Inc., 1936), 77.

2. C.S. Lewis, *Out of the Silent Planet* (New York: Macmillan, 1965; first paperback ed.), 136-37.

3. Etty Hillesum, *An Interrupted Life: The Diaries of Etty Hillesum 1941-43* , 2d ed. (New York: Washington Square Books, 1985), 107.

4. Ibid., 96.

5. Ibid., 119.

6. Ibid., 164.

7. Ibid., 100-1.

8. Ibid., 139.

9. Alphonsus Liguori, *The Incarnation, Birth, and Infancy of Jesus Christ*, ed. Eugene Grimm (Brooklyn/St. Louis/Toronto: Redemptorist Fathers, 1927), 360.

10. Thomas Merton, *No Man Is an Island* (Garden City, N.Y.: Image Books, 1955), 161.

11. Ibid., 163.

The Sixth Leg

1. *The Song of the Bird* (Garden City, N.Y.: Image Books, 1984), 153.

2. See *Lumen gentium*, nos. 8, 14-16 in Walter M. Abbot, gen. ed., *The Documents of Vatican II* (New York: Guild Press, 1966), 22-24, 32-35.

3. See *Lumen gentium*, nos. 9-17, *Unitatis redintegratio*, no. 9, *Nostrae aetate*, no. 2, *Digntatis humanae*, no. 1 in Abbot, gen. ed., *The Documents of Vatican II*, 24-37, 353, 662-63, 675.

4. Georges Bernanos, *The Diary of a Country Priest*, trans. Pamela Morris (New York: Macmillan, 1937; 1966 reprint), 97.

5. *Catechism of the Catholic Church*, par. 1439 (Vatican City: Libreria Editrice Vaticana, 1994), 361.

6. Gerard W. Hughes, *The God of Surprises* (London: Darton, Longmann and Todd, 1985; reprint, 1987), 154.

The Seventh Leg

1. *Joyce Kilmer's Anthology of Catholic Poets*, with a new Supplement by James Edward Tobin, revised ed. (Garden City, N.Y.: Image Books, 1955), 385-86.

2. Slavomir Rawicz, *The Long Walk: The True Story of a Trek to Freedom* (N.Y.: Lyons & Burford, 1956; reprint, 1984), 240.

3. Howard Higman, "Rings and Things" quoted in Dorothy C. Devers, *Faithful Friendship* (privately printed by the author, 1979; reprint, Cincinnati, Ohio: Forward Movement Publications, 1980, 1986), 41-44.

4. John Barth, *The Floating Opera*; quoted in Alvin Toffler, *Future Shock* (N.Y.: Random House, 1970), 93-94.

5. Cited in Toffler, *Future Shock*, 93-94.

6. Opinion of psychologist Courtney Tall, "Friendships in the Future;" quoted in Toffler, *Future Shock*, 93-94.

7. Newspaper clipping [source unknown].

8. These descriptions of affection, romantic love, and friendship come from C.S. Lewis, *The Four Loves* (San Diego, New York, London: Harcourt, Brace, Javanovich Publishers, 1960), 53, 96, 131.

9. Ibid., 184.

10. *Nicomachean Ethics*, 1156a7-1158b7.

11. *Nicomachean Ethics*, 1155b31-34, 1156a3-b12, 1170b5-10. The specific English terms come from Paul J. Wadell, *Friendship and the Moral Life* (Notre Dame, Ind.: University of Notre Dame Press, 1989), 130-31, 136-37.

12. *Summa Theologica*, II-II, q. 23, a. 1, resp.

13. Elizabeth A. Johnson, *She Who Is: The Mystery of God in Feminist Theological Discourse* (N.Y.: Crossroad, 1993), 216-17.

14. Aelred of Rievaulx, *Spiritual Friendship*, trans. Mary Eugenia Laker, with an Introduction by Douglas Roy, Cistercian Series 5 (Kalamazoo, Mich.: Cistercian Publications, 1977), 103.

15. Antoine de Saint Exupéry, *The Little Prince*, trans. Katherine Woods (N.Y., London: Harcourt, Brace, Javanovich, 1943; reprint, 1971), 83–84.

16. Aelred of Rievaulx, *Spiritual Friendship*, 104–5, 127.

17. Hugh Black, *Friendship* (Fleming H. Revell, Co., 1898), 219–37; quoted in Devers, *Faithful Friendship*, 5.

The Eighth Leg

1. Thomas Merton, *No Man Is an Island* (Garden City, N.Y.: Image Books, 1955), 165.

2. Alphonsus Liguori, *Prayer, The Great Means of Obtaining Salvation and All the Graces Which We Desire of God*, in *The Complete Works* vol. 3, p. 49.

3. Cf.   Athanasius of Alexandria, *De incarnatione*, 54.3 [*SC* 199:458–59; *PG* 25:191–92]; Gregory of Nyssa, *De opificio hominis*, 16 [*SC*, 6:151–61; *PG* 44:178–88].

4. Liguori, *Prayer*, 19, 201. The Alphonsus' title, "the great doctor of prayer," see Pius XI, "Allocuzione del 20 Settembre 1934," in *Annuarium Apostolatus Oraionis* (Rome, 1935), 73.

The Ninth Leg

1. From Oscar Williams, "The Last Supper," in *A Pocket Book of Modern Verse*, revised ed. (New York: Washington Square Press, 1958), 432.

The Final Leg

1. *Joyce Kilmer's Anthology of Catholic Poets*, with a new Supplement by James Edward Tobin, revised ed. (Garden City, N.Y.: Image Books, 1955), 334.

2. Shirley du Boulay, *The Road to Canterbury: A Modern Pilgrimage* (Great Britain: Harper Collins, 1994), 6.